AND THE T'WAIN SHALL MEET

AND THE T'WAIN SHALL MEET

By

PHYLLIS PISANO

This is a work of fiction. Any resemblance to characters, names, and otherwise is purely coincidental.

ISBN: 1-58721-799-6

1stBooks – rev. 10/30/00

About the Book

Trapped in a loveless marriage, Hatty, a shy and timid member of a powerful mid-west Ministry family is forced to marry the golden-haired, rising preacher, whose only reason for marrying her was to climb the ladder of success.

One day she witnesses his secret sex life and is totally destroyed.

She begins to blossom when the child of her husband's twin brother and his wife, killed by federal agents, comes to live with them.

Slowly she comes out of her shell and finds her body and soul in the unlikely person of Sonny Adams, a handsome and charismatic political consultant, who was born and raised on the streets of New York.

Hatty's life spins by as she fights her way out of and away from the rigid, repressive life allotted to her.

Her love revolves around the beautiful niece Violet; her brother Joshua, brilliant international lawyer and his lover, the Irish maid Mimi; Violet's love for the young, stunningly good-looking Vinny James whose destiny is headed for the entertainment world; Hatty's romance with the dashing Sonny; and the very beautiful Sicilian Gabriella who comes between Vinny and Violet.

Walk with them as they live through the twenties into the horrors of WW II.

Dedicated to
My mother Gracie and her sister Lena
who's story telling was the joy of our
childhood

1942

The stadium was packed. The band played. The singers chanted and the crowds roared as the golden-haired preacher with the seductive voice, the finely chiseled face that hinted of Michaelangelo's David; and his wife, a softly delicate pretty woman stepped up to the podium.

She gazed down at the adoring faces, ordinary people who became frenzied in their presence, were honoring the couple for standing up to the Government in declaring their conscientious objectors status.

The bombing of Pearl Harbor had thrown the nation into war and patriotism. All across the country the young men and women were throwing down their plows, so to speak, and marching off to war, but The Shepherds Followers, a ministry of avid pacifists, refused to bear arms.

The Reverend, the most vocal of the religious anti-war leaders, fearing that the sect would lose it's tax exempt benefits, came up with a brilliant scheme conceived in the name of God.

He raised his hands to silence the multitudes. When you could hear a pin drop in the vast arena, he swept his eyes across the crowd and in a soft and reverent voice began his speech.

"My dear brothers and sisters, he bowed his head, God has blessed us in a way only God can, to conquer and win our battle to refuse to bear arms against humanity."

The crowd screamed its approval.

"But," he continued, "It is our duty not only to serve God but also to serve God's children." He paused, scanned the crowd from left to right up to the balconies then raised his arms up to the sky and proclaimed, "As of today we are forming medical units, under the Followers banner to perform emergency and humane services on the battlefields around the world."

The crowd was stunned. The silence was deafening.

"We must be there," He continued, "To give emergency medical care to our soldiers, who were forced into this senseless conflict, comfort them, pray with them and show them that God loves them and is standing by their side."

1

A roar raced around the stadium with the force of thunder, showing their approval of this humane service being provided by the Shepherds Followers.

The pretty women smiled adoringly at her husband, the golden God. Underneath she was smoldering. 'You S.O.B. ' her inner self screamed. If this bunch only knew what you are really all about, they would not be bowing, scraping and adoring you. They would be booing and chasing you to the far corners of hell.

Mad as she was, she made sure they would never find out the real golden God because she held the winning card in her hands. That winning card gave her the leverage she needed to live outside the world she called a prison.

She smiled broadly. Oh how she hated this part of her life. A life of putting on a front, pretending, manipulating, deceiving, all this without a touch of love. A love so badly wanted and needed. A love she knew she could never have, but a love she was determined to find somewhere, somehow.

As the noise of the crowd swelled to a crescendo, she went back to the years when she was a born loser, the sparrow in a family of cardinals. A life so rigid, so devoid of laughter and joy that her heart cried openly in the still of the night when she shed the shield of pretending and obeying.

She looked out at the crowd and acknowledged their presence with a nod when she heard her husband proclaim That as of now, my beautiful wife is in charge of the Followers Units and will supervise the units wherever they will be.

What a nice way of getting me out of his hair, she thought, but I still hold the winning card. One false move and he won't even be a memory.

Her smile became broader with each roar of approval. It was a long journey from being a mouse who could barely squeak to a lion who knew how to roar.

1926

The Reverend Thorton Gilbert was bone tired. Stomping the Gospel route around the state was tough, hard work but the money rolled in and that was according to the plan.

He parked the long, black Packard touring car in the gravel driveway alongside the clapboard Victorian-style house. When he shut off the engine he realized there was a car parked at the curb.

Damn, He cursed. He was too tired to talk to anyone. All he wanted to do was soak in the tub and get some of the Kansas dust out of his lungs.

Hatty, his wife, met him at the screened door. This was a signal that someone of importance was inside. He looked at her blank face for a clue but the placid, meek features were bland.

She learned some things in the one year of her marriage to this dominating, ambitious preacher. One of them was never to let him see her emotions.

"Some people are in the parlor to see you," She whispered. He nodded, brushed past her and entered the formal, for visitors only, room off the center hall.

Two men, one with a Sheriff's badge pinned to his shirt, the other dressed in a black suit, rotating a Derby hat in his hands stood in the middle of the decorated room.

"Gentlemen," Thorton smiled and extended his hand to the man in the dark suit.

The man shook the preacher's hand, "Jack Blackton, Federal Agent. This is Sheriff Webster."

"I know the sheriff," Thorton smiled thinly, extending his hand to the local law man, thinking what the hell they wanted.

The Federal man cleared his throat, "I'm afraid I have some bad news."

The muscles under the preacher's eyes twitched slightly. He took a deep breath and looked at one and then the other to see if he could detect what there was that was so bad. His mind raced over the past weeks to see if he stepped out of the legal line. He couldn't find a single infraction.

He smiled "What could be so bad that the Lord can't mend?"

At twenty six years old, Thorton Gilbert was circuit preacher for the Shepherds Followers and a rising star. Blessed with good looks of an all-American male, he was dynamic and charismatic.

His plans for living were wealth, power and his own empire. He was working hard to make that dream come true and nothing was going to stop him.

He reserved his energy for his appearances on the podium. There his voice strong, resonant and seductive, easily lured the crowd into the palms of his hands. He preached the evils of alcohol, gambling, loose women and any indiscretion committed by a society gone mad.

This was the roaring twenties and he was roaring towards his dream.

The Federal man cleared his throat nervously and forced his voice out of parched lips. "Reverend, it's your brother Preston."

"Oh yes," Thorton sighed, What's he up to now? Damn that brother of mine he cursed under his breath, he's in trouble again.

Preston Gilbert was Thorton's twin brother. They were identical in looks and bearing. Both had wheat-colored hair, steel-blue eyes and rugged chiseled features.

They grew up poor. Genteel poor. Their father was a Minister whose ideology and poor business administrations kept them on the peripheral of the economic and social ladder.

Their mother took to her bed most of the time. It was her escape from disappointment. She paid so little attention to the boys, they raised themselves through the difficult growing-up years.

As twins they should have been close but their personalities were in constant conflict. Preston was easy-going and fun – loving. Thorton was ambitious and scheming. Both had the ability to charm and they each used this gift for their own purposes.

At eighteen, Preston packed a bag and left to find a place in the sun.

Their parent's heartbreak was a bitter pill for Thorton to swallow.

The agent lowered his eyes and focused his gaze on one of the flower patterns woven in the rug. He hated this part of his job. Most of the times he would deliver the terrible news quickly and try for a hasty retreat.

This situation called for a more delicate delivery. He cleared his throat, "He's dead," The words rushed out. "His wife too."

"Dead? Wife? What are you talking about?" His mind went back a few years when Preston showed up at their parent's Oklahoma house with a Eurasian girl clinging to his arm. Nothing unusual for Preston, the lazy, no-good womanizer." What do you want?" Thorton raged, "I don't want you here."

Preston laughed uproariously," My dear sainted brother," he stopped laughing and a sneer crossed his face." I have no intention of staying in this tacky, shabby house."

Thorton's features relaxed as his brother continued," I just stopped by on my way to the Florida Keys. I came to pick up some things I left in the attic."

Thorton smiled slyly," Anything that was in the attic was thrown out long ago."

Preston shrugged his shoulders, "No matter, the stuff would've left a bad taste in my mouth."

He turned to leave. As he approached the door, he swung around and grinned broadly," If you ever need anything, dear brother, call me in care of romance and adventure, Florida Keys, U.S.A."

Thorton stood in the shabby parlor fuming," That's what you think dear brother, if anything you'll need me."

The air hung still in the richly colored room. Thorton turned his head and looked at the painting of his father hanging over the fireplace. The Federal agent waited.

Preston could almost see the tears falling down the Minister's cheeks. A man, who to him, was humble, pious and stupid. A man whose tears flowed for everyone's troubles but his own. He turned around and said quietly, "Please sit down."

The agent sat down in a winged chair flanking the fireplace. Thorton sat in the other and faced him.

"Please tell me what happened," The muscles rigid in his face, "And don't spare the details."

The agent gave him an apologetic look. "Reverend, your brother was a rum runner."

Thorton's head bounced against the back of the chair in agony. "My brother was many things Mr. Blackton," Thorton's eyes narrowed, "But breaking the law was something my family never committed."

The agent's voice took on a hard edge." He was running the stuff from Cuba to the Keys. We were watching the boat, which was part of a fishing fleet and trailed it back to port."

Thorton's eyes narrowed into two slits. The man swallowed hard, "We waited until the boat docked, then raided it. We had our guns drawn, we had to defend ourselves. He fired first."

Thorton's muscles in his body tightened . He knew that by nightfall he would be suffering one of his tormenting migraines.He spoke in a strained voice, "I know how difficult it was for you to bring me this news but my brother did pretty much what he wanted to do. If he lived by the gun then the Lord willed it he die by the gun."

He closed his eyes indicating a silent prayer.

The agent cleared his throat again. "That's not the whole story Reverend." He swallowed hard, the whole incident played in his mind over and over sending shivers up and down his spine.

It was at a Florida Keys marina. He remembered that for several minutes the air was filled with the sounds of machine guns. Then everything went quiet. Silence hung in the air like a thick mantle broken only by the gentle slapping water against the hull of the boat.

The Federal men waited five more minutes then warily climbed aboard the old fishing vessel. They searched the deck and found a man sprawled on his back, a machine gun clutched in his hand. Lying almost on top of him was a woman, her hands grasping his arm as if she was engaged in a desperate attempt to stop him.

The chief signaled to another agent and they warily descended the stairs to the galley. A pot of fish stew, still warm, was on the stove. Three soup plates and three spoons were placed on the small table.

The two men looked at each other. Fear crossed their features. There was another person on board. The chief nodded to his companion. They cocked their guns and inched their way to a door at the far end of the room. They positioned themselves on each side of the door frame. The chief took a deep breath, rushed the door and yelled "Freeze."

No sound came from the darkened room. He backed up, felt along the wall for a light switch and flipped it on. A pool of light brought the room into focus. He quickly scanned the tiny cubicle.

A bed piled with quilts and a built-in dresser filled the small hold. Suddenly the quilt moved. He aimed his gun and shouted, "Come out with your hands up."

The quilt moved again. The bed covers slowly folded back. The men triggered for action, gasped with astonishment, when the face of the enemy appeared above the quilts.

Thorton opened his eyes and sighed, "I'll take care of the arrangements if that's what 's bothering you."

"Oh no Sir," The man moved his body around in the chair, "There's another matter that needs your attention."

"Oh?" The preacher's eyes narrowed. What else could this man have to tell him. His brother was dead. Good riddance to a blight that began the day the two brothers were old enough to play and Preston always managed to outwit and outfox his twin.

The Federal man coughed. "He left a little girl Reverend. She's about three years old."

Thorton was dumbfounded.

"You're her only relative," The man blurted.

Hatty was down in the basement standing next to the chimney listening to every word that was being said upstairs.

The chimney was built to heat the parlor and bedroom above it. Every word that was said in the parlor filtered down the chimney and into the basement.

She discovered this the first day they moved into the big Victorian house. She had gone down to the basement to store some boxes. Thorton was in the parlor directing the moving men where to put the furniture.

"Place the wing chairs next to the fireplace," His voice filtered down. "A little closer," He instructed, "I like to be near the person I'm conversing with."

She heard the movements of the chairs, then the voice of one of the moving men boom down the chimney, "I'll bet you talk to a lot of people."

"Yes I do." Thorton answered, his voice clear as crystal.

Hatty was always curious about the workings of the Shepherds Followers. Thorton never discussed any of the Ministry's details with her, so from that day on when her husband and staff talked behind the closed parlor door, Hatty went down to the basement, stood next to the chimney and heard everything.

Thorton looked at the agent and did what he tried very hard not to do. He lost his composure. He bounded out of the chair and stood over the man. His features flaming with anger, shouted, "What do you mean, I'm his only relative?"

His arms flailed the air, "Four years ago he showed up with an Asian woman. Those people breed like flies she must have lots of relatives."

He went back to his chair and sat down, "Go find them, the way you found me."

The man straightened up and answered softly, "We checked with the International Police."

"And?" Thorton's voice came down a decibel.

"Your brother's wife was the daughter of a French-Chinese woman and a Russian father-a white Russian."

The man paused and cleared his throat then continued," Her parents were political activists working out of Shanghai. One night they were ambushed on a dark, little traveled road. Your brother's wife was sixteen at the time."

The man paused and cleared his throat again, "There are no relatives. All their associates fled."

The preacher shifted uneasily in his chair. The man continued, "She was alone. She lived wherever she could. She was a beautiful girl. Men wanted her."

Thorton snorted, "Naturally, what did you expect, a paragon of virtue?"

"Your brother," The Federal agent continued, "Rescued her from a bad fight. He took her home with him. Shortly after they left Shanghai without a trace."

Silence permeated the room. Thorton looked at the man and wondered what was coming next? "What do you want from me Mr. Blacton?" His voice showing the strain.

The man leaned over and whispered, "What any good Christian would do. Take the child to live with you. Here she'll have a decent, God-fearing home."

The agent took a deep breath, "If you don't take her she will be placed in an orphanage."

Two weeks later Hatty and Thorton were standing on the broad veranda when the Government car pulled up in front of the house.

Thorton's face was pale. A nerve from his neck to his temple twitched uncontrollably. Hatty stood by his side, her face frozen, her shoulders high.

From the moment they knew that Preston's child was coming to live with them a charged electrical currant ran the Gilbert household.

Thorton fought the rage that engulfed him. The migraines were frequent. Preaching was the only relief he felt in a situation that was tearing him apart.

Hatty went about her duties with a face that showed no emotions.

He stormed about the house shouting, "I expect her to behave or both of you will feel the brunt of my wrath."

Hatty lowered her eyes and nodded her head obediently.

The car door opened. A big man got out and looked up at the couple. Thorton nodded his head.

The man reached into the recess of the car and brought out the child.

Thorton and Hatty gasped. The tiny figure was topped with a thick, luxurious mane that went down to her waist like a shimmering sheath of gold.

Her face was buried in the man's shoulder. He held her closely as if to comfort her and came up the walk. An officious-looking woman carrying a paper bag followed.

When they reached the steps, the man whispered gently into the child's ear, "You're home now Violet...home with Uncle Thorton and Aunt Hatty."

The little girl buried her head deeper into the man's shoulder.

Thorton and Hatty stood transfixed.

Suddenly Hatty went down the steps and said quietly, "I'll take her."

She put her hands gently on the child's arms and said, "It's alright child."

Violet picked up her head and looked at the woman. Her small oval face, tanned by the sun was dominated by almond-shaped eyes the color of smoky wood violets.

She then turned her gaze to the handsome, blond man and a bright look of recognition crossed her face.

She stretched out her arms and cried, "Daddy."

Thorton recoiled as if he had been hit with a brick. The little girl recoiled back into the big man's arms.

Hatty took the child and cradled her in a loving embrace.

Thorton remained frozen. He was too shocked to move.

Hatty carried Violet into the house whispering endearments into the child's ear.

Thorton composed himself and thanked the man for his kindness into seeing that Preston and his wife were buried in the Florida Keys.

The officious woman stepped forward and handed him the paper bag. "Not much in here. Just a doll, some hair ribbons, a photograph and one," She held up one finger, "Change of clothing."

A smirk crossed her mouth, "Your brother traveled lightly."

Thorton winced. "She'll be well clothed and fed here."

The woman's face softened. "Love her a little bit too, Reverend."

The agent turned quickly and left. The woman followed but kept looking back at the steely-eyed man on the veranda.

The car roared away in a cloud of dust. Thorton watched it disappear. His body quivered with anger. He turned and entered the house.

Hatty and Violet were seated on the sofa, the child huddled against her. Thorton went and stood over them, his rage now distorting his features.

"Violet? What kind of name is that?"

Hatty's lips trembled. "Asian people name their children after flowers."

"That's what you get from a bunch of heathens," Thorton roared. "Women of ill-repute are named after flowers."

Hatty tightened her grip on the child. Thorton walked back and forth, his head bent in concentration.

The two females, one a timid nineteen year old woman, the other a frightened three year old, looked on in terrified silence.

After an interminable time, he stopped short. He took a hard look at the little girl then turned to his wife, "From now on, she," Pointing a finger at Violet," Will be registered and known as Livinia Elisabeth Gilbert, after my mother, who is probably turning over in her grave right now, her grandmother," pointing a finger at the child.

He turned from them and held his head between his hands as if in deep pain. "That's the best we can do for her."

Hatty took the child's hand and the paper bag and left the room quietly. She carried the child up the broad staircase, the tiny head buried in her neck.

Once inside the bedroom, she gently closed the door and placed the child on the big, ornately carved bed.

She put her hands on the little girl's head and lovingly stroked the long, silken hair.

"You're beautiful Violet," The shy timid woman whispered, "And I'm so glad you've come to live with us."

The child kept her face down.

Hatty opened the paper bag and lifted out a richly, carved ivory framed picture. Violet quickly grabbed the frame and hugged it to her body.

Hatty smiled. "May I see it?"

The child hesitated then slowly showed the photo to Hatty. It was a picture of Preston with his arms around a pretty girl. Her features were sleek and lean. Her neck was incredibly long and her eyes terribly sad.

"My God," Hatty exclaimed, She resembles a Gauguin painting.

The child pointed to Preston, "Daddy," then pointed to the woman, "Maman."

The child looked like Preston with his all-American look but the eyes, despite their color, were the eyes of the Orient.

This child is going to be something, thought the plump, timid woman.

She placed her hand under the girl's chin, "Uncle Thorton is a very stern man. We must do whatever he tell us."

The child did not respond.

"But you needn't worry about him," She said as her hands played with the child's hair. " I'll show you how to play a very special game." A smile curved the corners of her mouth. "Yes my darling little Violet, a very special game."

Chapter Two

Hatty Howell Gilbert was an obscure woman. Her presence went unnoticed by the people who surrounded her husband. The dynamic personality of Thorton Gilbert overshadowed everyone, including important, influential men. When Hatty stood by his side she was reduced to nothing.

She grew up under the stern thumb of her father, the Reverend Isaiah Holwell, regional head of he Society of the Good Shepherds in south central Kansas.

She learned at an early age to keep out of the way of grown-ups; to keep her emotions to herself and never, ever show her temper.

"Enter the room quietly." Her mother continually admonished.

"You must be a lady at all times," She was reminded.

"Don't speak above a whisper," She was advised, "Or People will think you are vulgar. Yes, Mamma," She would meekly reply.

Children were reluctant to play with the Minister's daughter. She was never invited to other children's parties and never asked to participate in their games.

Many times she heard them taunt, "Hatty is a scaredy cat. Hatty is a mamma's girl."

Circumstances forced her to become a loner. Her only ally in this formidable atmosphere was her brother Joshua, two years her senior.

He was given more freedom. He was male and expected to occupy an important place in the Followers organization.

He was good natured and easy-going but he possessed an uncanny intelligence that put him in an important position in the Holwell household.

He loved his sister. She was the sparrow in a family of cardinals and he understood her frustration of subjugation.

He would spend time with her whenever he could. He would take her to the meadow, a distance behind their house, settle down under a tree to study thus giving Hatty the freedom to play and shout without Mamma reprimanding her.

A strong bond developed between brother and sister. He often told her that people would bully her and she better find her own way of fighting back.

She didn't understand him. She didn't know the meaning of the word 'bully' even though she was bullied all the time by her parents and schoolmates.

With each passing year she retreated deeper into the world of fantasy. There she was the leader and all faces turned towards her adoringly.

With each fantasy she buried the anger of restriction deeper into the recess of her mind.

'Someday' she dreamed, 'I'll fly, free as a bird. I'll fly to the ends of the earth. There will be no one to tell me what to do.'

It was these dreams that carried the genteel, pretty, slightly plump Hatty through to the destiny of her life.

One day she was summoned to her father's study. A tiny bell ominously tolled inside her head. Fear overtook her.

'Why did her father want to see her in his study? It has to be of utmost importance. All directives from him were issued through her mother. He spoke to her only at the dinner table with a terse statement about her studies or her music lessons. She played the piano and the organ.

At the age of fourteen, she was put in front of the organ in her father's church five minutes before Sunday services and was informed that she was now the church's organist.

The young girl was horror stricken. She stared at her mother. She tried to protest but her vocal chords froze.

Her mother firmly straightened the girl's shoulders and without any compassion said, "You're ready."

The frightened girl looked at the people around her for a friendly face. No one seemed to notice her. She felt the world crumbling around her. Her only resource was to flee-a compulsive act- for a highly disciplined girl.

She was so scared, she was about to run when she saw the smiling face of her brother.

He had just entered the church. She gave him a pleading look. He winked. He always winked when he knew she was disturbed. It had a calming effect.

She bowed her head, sucked in her breath and played like a dutiful daughter.

At sixteen she began the arduous study of sign language, her father's favorite project-The Followers School For The Deaf.

The Reverend Howell was an astute man. This was the core of his ministry. This was the money raiser. Keeping the deaf community in the public's eye kept the church's coffers overflowing.

She was eighteen now. 'What' she thought did her father have in store for her? With her heart beating wildly, Hatty knocked softly on the door of her father's study. A terse, sharp voice answered the knock.

He was seated behind his huge rosewood desk. It was an ornate and expensive piece of furniture, imported from Brazil, with intricate carvings dominating the reddish, black streaked wood. Papers were spread over the top,

She stood there waiting for him to look up from his work.

'Maybe' She thought, I'm going to start teaching the deaf children, instead of just helping the teachers. Her mind started tripping over past events. She was so nervous everything blurred into one unrecognizable cloud.

"Don't stand there like a statue," He ordered, his eyes still scanning the papers." Sit down,"

She lowered herself into the big oversized armchair facing the desk, her feet just barely reaching the thick Karistan rug.

"Well Hatty," Her father finally raised his head and looked at her," You're eighteen years old now, it's time you got married."

His words hit her with the speed of lightening.

She bolted out of the chair, "Married?" The words flew out of her throat burning her vocal chords. She gasped and coughed.

A look of amusement played on the Reverend's face. "Yes," He smiled, "And please sit down."

Hatty sank into the big chair, her eyes riveted in panic to her father's face.

"Who?" She whispered. Her hands went to her throat and began to message her neck as if to ease a terrible pain.

What was her father doing to her? All the young men she knew were away at school. Besides they all had pimples on terribly ugly faces. She took a deep breath and got some courage from within.

"Please Father ," She pleaded, "I don't want to get married. At least not yet.

The stern face lost its smile. "Of course you do. A girl of eighteen should be married. It'll keep her out of trouble."

She gasped. "Father, I've never given you any trouble."

"True," He answered, "But you've reached the age where the best place for you is besides a husband."

"Father, I don't know of anyone I want to marry."

"You don't have to," He replied matter-of-factly, "I've chosen a very suitable young man for you."

Her hands went to her throat again. Tears welled up in her soft amber eyes.

He ignored her anguish.

"The young man I've chosen," He continued, "Is a very capable, promising young minister. He is definitely on his way to prominence. You will have a good life."

Her voice wavered out of quivering lips, "What's his name? Do I know him?"

Her father waved his hand in dismissal and said curtly, "You will meet him tonight at dinner."

'Why didn't her mother warn her', She wondered. She could have told her or at least give her a hint when Hatty noticed her mother carefully checking the china, glassware and table linens.

"Are we having guests for dinner this evening?" Hatty asked.

"Yes," Her mother answered with a tight-lipped look, "And you will be on your best behavior."

"Mother," Hatty teased, "When am I never well behaved?"

"When you and your brother are up to something," The tight corseted woman huffed.

"But mother," She wailed defensively.

16

"Never mind," the stern face interrupted, "Tend to your chores."

Hatty left for classes and completely forgot the incident. Now it all came back to her like a hot prairie wind.

"You may go now," Her father ordered, "Dinner is at eight." The stern, uncompromising face went back to his papers.

Hatty went to her room and softly closed the door behind her. She leaned against the carved panels and allowed the anger to come to the surface. She dashed to the bed and threw herself on the patch-work quilt and buried her head into the softness of the lambs-wool mattress. There she muffled the sobs that wracked her body.

Why were they doing this to her? What were they afraid of? Had they noticed her distraction when the older brother of one of the deaf pupils came to pick up his little sister?

He was very handsome with dark, curly hair and eyes the color of a clear blue sky. Hatty couldn't take her eyes off him.

Perhaps one of the teachers told her mother about him. She heard this teacher describe him as one of those eyetalians that came to the territory to build the new roads.

They weren't taking any chances with their daughter straying from the fold.

And who was this man they had picked for her? She stopped crying and sat up. Fantasy pushed her anger aside. Who indeed, was the young minister her father was considering as his son-in-law?

Once a month a young student from the Theological College participated in the Sunday Services. Not one of them stood out in her mind.

'Maybe, just maybe,' She thought, 'He might be the handsome gallant who will carry her away from this awful, restricted house and settle her into a fruitful, active household. There she would reign as the supreme hostess, always by her husband's side, giving him the advise she knew he needed.

She dressed carefully. After much deliberation she decided on a pastel pink flowered batiste dress with puff sleeves. The narrow waist accentuated her firm, full bosom giving her the look of a ripe peach.

17

She dusted her face with powder, the only make-up she was allowed to have, pinched her cheeks and bit her lips to give them color.

She piled her hair up on her head and pinned it to keep it under control. But tendrils of light-brown curls released themselves against her face adding a slightly naughtiness to her appearance.

She twirled in front of the Cheval mirror appraising herself and smiled. 'I am pretty.' She thought. She hoped her suitor would approve too.

She waited on top of the staircase, where she could not be seen. Voices drifted upward.

The guests were arriving. "Do not come down," Her mother cautioned, "Until I send for you."

The guests were in the drawing room, drinking lemonade. Mimi, the Irish immigrant maid came up the stairs to summon her down.

She was a big strapping girl, twenty years old, and had been with the Holwells only two weeks. She moved cautiously in this strict, religious household, saying little and absorbing everything.

Her heart went out to the sparrow of this formidable family. 'They're crushing her for sure,' She said to herself and felt the suffocation of the young girl.

Hatty on the other hand was fascinated by the big girl with the fiery red hair that refused to be restrained.

The Holwells hired her as an act of Christian duty. The wave of immigrants flooded the nation with unskilled, uneducated people, thereby creating a glut of cheap labor.

The rich and penurious grabbed these people with an inborn greed and felt virtuous in their charity.

The Holwells saw in Mimi a big, strong female who could do heavy duty work. They paid her five dollars a month plus room and board and referred to her as the Irish char girl and kept her out of sight.

Mimi smiled at Hatty, "You're looking very pretty, lassie," Her Irish lilt soft and melodious.

"Do you think so," Whispered the frightened Hatty.

Mimi put her hands on the young girl's shoulders, "Don't let the dragons frighten you lassie, they're only in your mind."

She patted her on the shoulders, "Go downstairs, smile and the dragons will go away."

Hatty hugged her, straightened her shoulders and descended the staircase.

She entered the drawing room hesitantly. Her rapidly beating heart reverberated on her eardrums, erasing all other sounds. She kept her eyes down, terrified of what she would discover.

Her father's voice, now purring smoothly, dimmed the beating in her ears.

"Gentlemen, this is my daughter Hatty."

She curtsied. Her eyes still downcast, she scanned the polished shoes of the men. She could tell a great deal about people by looking at their feet. This was a game she developed to a science in the years she spent on top of the stairs looking down at her parent's visitors.

She could only see feet from her viewing spot behind the potted plant. She could tell if they were young or old, tall or short, lean or fat. She could even tell if they were dull or spirited.

Her eyes rested for a moment on a youthful pair of shoes then slowly made their way up to the face.

The body was strong and muscular. An athlete? The shoulders were broad. The neck powerful and strong.

Then her eyes rested on his face. A slight gasp escaped from her lips. The face was strong and handsome with features that looked as if they were chiseled from marble.

Steel-blue eyes stared down at her. A smile curled his lips. A slight chill brushed her body. Goosebumps appeared all over her arms.

He extended his hand and his voice, deep and melodious filled the room.

"Reverend Thorton Gilbert, Circuit Preacher of the Southern District."

She gave him her hand. A soft but powerful hand enclosed her. The words tumbled out in a rush, "Pleased to meet you Reverend."

She lowered her eyes, 'Oh thank you Father,' She murmured to herself, 'Thank you for the wonderful gift.'

They sat across each other at dinner. Making conversation with him was awkward. She didn't mind, it gave her the opportunity to observe the man who would soon be her husband.

Throughout dinner he held the attention of the other guests, all members of the Clergy. They leaned towards him and listened rapturously to every word.

He's so wondrously handsome, her heart sang. Then a terrible thought crossed her mind. What if it's one of the other men who are old. Then she remembered her Father's words in the study (he's a very capable, promising young minister.)

The other men were established in their own churches. The Reverend Gilbert was a Circuit Preacher. Her heart sang again and Hatty settled down to dinner weaving her web of fantasy.

Every now and then she looked up at the shining knight who was going to make her dreams come true.

Once she caught him looking at her. Her cheeks blushed with color. She quickly lowered her eyes.

After dinner the men retired to the study. Hatty and her Mother went into the drawing room. Mrs. Holwell sat down to her needlepoint. Hatty sat down at the massive grand piano.

'Soon,' Hatty's heart sang, 'Soon she would leave the restricted life of the Holwell family. She would be the wife of the traveling preacher.

She would go everywhere with him. She would make him so proud of her. In the glow of fantasy her fingers went into the first bars of Mozart's "Seduction Duet".

She smiled dreamily. "Mamma, do you think I'm pretty?"

The woman didn't answer.

"Mamma," the young girl stopped playing. Her mother gave her a thoughtful look, pursed her lips and stated, "You have nice features."

The disappointed Hatty hunched her body. "Don't pout," Her mother admonished, "He must see something in you, he made a formal request to marry you."

"He made a formal request?" The delighted girl jumped up from her seat. "But Mamma we never met."

The older woman kept her eyes on her needlework, "He's been aware of you for a long time."

"He has?" Hatty stood in front of her mother, totally unaware she was breaking a house rule of etiquette, that she must never confront her parents with rebuttal. Her mother looked up at her daughter who was blushing furiously.

"He saw you the first day you became the Church's organist, four years ago. If you hadn't been so foolishly frightened, you would have noticed him."

"Mother, I was only fourteen years old."

Her mother put her needlework down, "You made an impression on a fine young man," The older woman retorted, "You can thank the Lord for that."

The young girl was too flabbergasted to continue.

Her mother folded her needlework and rose from the chair. "Come, we shall bid the gentlemen goodnight and retire to our rooms."

Mrs. Holwell knocked softly on the massive door of the study, opened it and entered with her daughter behind her.

The three guests were seated around the huge desk. Reverend Howell was seated in his throne-of-a-chair.

Hatty couldn't help noticing that he looked like a king holding court but the handsome young prince was filling the room with his golden presence making the king look old and tired.

Joy filled her heart.

The men rose from their chairs.

"We've come to bid you goodnight, " Mrs. Holwell sang. Her voice always sang for guests.

Hatty curtsied and stole another look at the young man who had come to ask for her hand in marriage.

He extended his hand, "Good night Miss Hatty, may I have the pleasure of your company after this Sunday's Services?"

"Yes," She breathed softly, "After services on Sunday."

Her mother, gently but firmly, took her arm and ushered her out of the room.

Sunday took forever. Hatty walked on a cloud. Her mother scolded her frequently. She paid very little attention.

Suddenly she was in love. 'So this is what it's like,' She sang. The world turned rosier by the hour.

Finally the big day arrived and the young girl started to experience the jitters.

'Oh I hope I don't hit any sour notes this morning,' She cried to herself, he'll never come back. He'll think I'm so stupid.'

She dressed carefully and when she was satisfied with her appearance, she went downstairs and waited for her mother.

The older woman checked the young girl's dress and pulled up the bodice so that the ruffle around the collar covered more of Hatty's neck.

She sat down at the organ waited for the services to begin. She could feel the perspiration rolling down her back.

Suddenly the side door to the altar opened and her father entered the Church. Following him was the Reverend Thorton Gilbert, Hatty's golden God.

Her heart leapt against her chest beating rapidly. Her father glanced at her and signaled for her to begin.

Hatty played as she never played before. The joy within her coursed down to her fingers and the music filled the Church with a renewed spirit.

She gazed rapturously at the young Reverend as his strong, moving voice preached the sermon of the day.

'Oh yes,' She sang to herself, "You are so very, very promising and so very, very handsome.

Her mother did not leave the young couple alone at all that Sunday afternoon. They sat in the drawing room sipping lemonade before dinner.

When Thorton asked Hatty a question, her mother answered for her. Hatty didn't mind. She was so enraptured with the newness of the idea of marrying and living a new life, she forgave the older woman.

'Let Mother talk all she wants,' She comforted herself, 'Soon we will be together and alone.'

Then a terrifying thought descended upon her, 'What do men and women do when they go to bed?'

Lately the strange stirrings within her were so powerful they frightened her...especially when she thought of her golden prince.

She envisioned him totally naked. He resembled a marble statue she had seen in an art picture book-rippling muscles, chiseled features and a huge bulge between his legs covered with a leaf.

She was confused. Then she brightened. The vision changed to a knight who came charging into her house, swept her off her feet and took her away.

After a three month courtship, Hatty and Thorton were married.

During that time, Hatty saw very little of her golden prince. Wedding preparations took up every minute of the day.

Her mother kept her busy from morning 'till night with fittings, invitation lists, reception menu and wedding gifts that poured in from her parent's friends and colleagues.

The whirlwind activities made Hatty tired, bewildered and sometimes very frightened.

She so desperately wanted to spend time alone with her new love. She wanted to touch him. To run her fingers through his wheat-colored hair. She wanted him to put his arms around her and hold her close, just like lovers in the romance novels she kept hidden in the basement.

She wanted him to unlace her bodice slowly while he looked into her eyes and let the night envelope them in ecstasy. Her dreams were full of fantasies.

The wedding was a pompous affair. Important and influential members of the Clergy from all over the state were present.

Most of Hatty's relatives were either in the ministry, law or banking.

She did not notice all the power gathered around her that day. All she could think of was the golden prince ready to whisk her away.

Her mother gave her so many instructions she had difficulty trying to remember them.

To add to the confusion, her cousin Mathilda, famous for her sharp, acerbic tongue was her maid-of-honor.

They were in Hatty's bedroom putting on the finishing touches to their faces when Mathilda blurted, "I swear Hatty, you must have practiced witchcraft to get yourself such a catch."

She poked the bride in the stomach, "Come on, tell me, what did you do?"

Hatty blushed furiously. She never liked Mathilda. She always felt very uncomfortable around the brash, outspoken cousin.

Hatty was happy they lived a hundred miles apart.

Mathilda twirled in front of the full-length mirror, appraised herself and smiled. Then she turned around and sat on the edge of the bed next to Hatty.

"Just think," She cooed, "Tonight you will be in bed with a man. A big, beautiful, strong man."

She poked Hatty in the stomach again, "You are such a mouse, I guess when Thorton jumps on top of you and tries you know what, you'll scream bloody murder."

Hatty looked horrified. "Whatever do you mean by 'you know what?"

"Oh come on," Mathilda roared, "Don't act like such an innocent."

"I really don't know what you mean," Terror showing in the amber eyes.

Mathilda realized Hatty was telling the truth and maliciously decided to tell the bride the intimate details of a wedding night.

"First," she gleefully whispered, "He will rip the clothes right off your body."

Hatty stood up and backed away from the wicked words this horrible girl just uttered.

Her cousin went on and became very animated by playing charade, "Then he will throw you on the bed, jump on you, push that big thing between his legs between your legs and make a big hole in your body. Then you'll just bleed and bleed."

The color drained from Hatty's face turning it as white as her dress.

She stared in horror at her cousin whose face wore a satisfied and smug look.

The door opened and the Reverend and Mrs. Holwell entered. Her father took her arm and said, "It's time to go."

The guests watched the powerful Reverend escort the numb bride down the staircase and into the drawing room where her uncle the Reverend Jonathan Holwell was waiting with the young groom.

The rest of the day went by in a blur. Events and people crowded in and out of her mind like a revolving door, seeing but not seeing, listening but not hearing.

Finally the bride and groom, now dressed in their going-away outfits left the reception and were driven by Hatty's brother and a cousin to a lodge on a near-by lake just over the Kansas border to begin their new life together.

It was an hour's drive and the shy bride sat mute in the seat next to her husband.

When at last they were alone in their honeymoon chamber, Thorton let out a whistle, "Thank God that's over."

"Oh yes," She replied, "Thank God it's over."

She sat on the edge of bed and waited. Suddenly she wasn't nervous anymore. She was free. Free from her sharp, terse parents. Free now to be her own person. An adult to be looked up to and respected.

Thorton went to the window and stood there looking out into the night.

Hatty watched her brand new husband and saw lovers from her novels taking off their clothes and melting into each other's arms.

She stood up quickly, took off her skirt and blouse. She picked up her petticoat and unhooked the garters from her stockings. She removed her shoes and stockings. She was standing now in her laced bodice and petticoat waiting for him to come over.

He turned around, looked her up and down and gave her a hard look. He went to the wardrobe and with his back turned to her, began undressing.

She watched fascinated. First his jacket came off, then his tie and shirt.

She clutched her hands to the bedpost as he unbuttoned his pants. Her eyes never left him.

As he pulled off his under shorts he said wearily, "Remove your garments, we might as well get this over with."

She obeyed but kept her eyes riveted to his body.

With his back still turned from her he kept his eyes on the window.

His body gleamed gloriously. He turned around and Hatty gasped.

Placed between his legs was not the big, ugly thing, cousin Mathilda said he had, but a limp appendage that looked more like a thumb.

'Oh thank God,' Hatty sighed in relief, 'he is not the monster Mathilda said he was.

They went to bed and he pulled the covers over them.

He quickly got on top of her and before she knew what was happening, he was off and on to his side of the bed.

"This is the first and last time we will indulge in this sinful lust," His voice tinged with a hard edge. "Now let us both pray to the Almighty God to cleanse our souls so that our spirits will always be ready to be received in Heaven.

Hatty meekly prayed with her husband while hot, salty tears rolled down her face as the strange stirrings in her loins roared.

The young couple settled in their new home. He busied himself with his preaching, she ran the household and whenever she could she would escape down to the basement where she kept all the romance novels she could get her hands on.

Chapter Three

The simple act of making Hatty his wife opened all the doors Thorton wanted to enter.

His smooth, resonant voice mesmerized the multitudes. His aloof bearing, his stunning good looks added an aura of mystery and underlying power.

He drove women wild. He had his eyes on the stars and he wasn't going to let any woman take it away from him.

Because he didn't succumb to these temptations his followers assumed he was madly in love with his wife.

He could barely tolerate Hatty. He found her timid and repressed. He had to force himself to remember that she held the key to his success.

They shared the same house but he could barely share the same bed with her.

He was always somewhere preaching or at a meeting. Occasionally he would bring some important people home.

Hatty would serve sumptuous dinners and hope that Thorton would somehow remember she was his wife.

Once while visiting her mother, she dared to mention that Thorton was never home and when he was, he never paid any attention to her.

Her mother's wrath stunned her deeply. "Be thankful that you are married to a handsome, promising young preacher. Women are not supposed to be happy and catered to."

Hatty cringed as her mother continued, "Lots of beautiful girls will go to all length to have what you have."

Hatty never mentioned it again.

Life moved slowly for the lonely woman. Her only solace was in the romance novels she buried herself in and imagined herself as the heroin.

At night before going to bed she would get a book and read until she fell asleep, the book lying open on her bed.

In the morning she would dash down to the basement and put the novel away. She didn't want the daily cleaning woman to know her secret.

On the nights Thorton was home, she would quickly remove the bedding the following morning from the leather sofa in the study, where he always slept.

His excuse for sleeping there was that he could work all night without disturbing her.

It had been a frustrating day. The cleaning woman's son came over and told her his mother was sick in bed and couldn't come over for a couple of days.

She was relying on the woman to help her overhaul the linen room.

No matter. She would take care of the necessary chores first then start on the room in the afternoon.

She had just finished her lunch when she heard a car pull up under the portico. She went to the window and saw Thorton climbing the steps.

'What a strange time to be coming home,' Thought Hatty.

He walked into the foyer and hung his coat. Hatty entered the room and asked concernedly, "Is anything wrong?"

"Why should anything be wrong?" His handsome face showing fatigue.

Her words stumbled over each other. "Well you never come home this hour of the day."

His eyes narrowed. "Did I interrupt something?"

"Oh no," She replied. Did she see a sign of jealousy? Hope welled within her.

He turned his back and headed for the study. "I have some matters to take care of. I'll be in my study. I don't wish to be disturbed."

"Of course," She answered. All her hope disintegrated to dust.

"Would you like some lunch first?" Hope returning to her.

"I'm not hungry." He turned his back and entered the study closing the door behind him.

Hatty returned to the kitchen and poured herself a cup of coffee.

'How' She thought ,'Can I make him notice me?'

Tears rolled down her cheeks. All these strange feeling stirring within her. Feelings of longing to be held in strong gentle arms. Warm kisses caressing her lips. Restless hands exploring her body.

What Hatty and Thorton did on their wedding night was not what happened in her novels. Lovers were united and became one. The world faded away and was replaced by heaven in all its glory.

What had she done wrong to be treated this way?

If only there was someone she could talk to. The thought made her shudder. Women just didn't talk that way. At least not in her circle of acquaintances.

'Yes,' She thought, 'There is somebody she could talk to. She would gather all the courage she needed and talk to her husband . It was their problem and they were the only ones who could solve it.'

She decided to let it rest. She would start work in the linen room, then make a delicious dinner…soften and mellow him with good food and then discuss the problem.

The linen room was the size of a small bedroom. One door led to the hallway and another to the bathroom which was situated between the linen room and the master bedroom.

Moving quietly, Hatty entered the linen room and closed the door. It was bright with sunshine streaming through the large window.

She always felt a terrible sadness when she entered this room.

The builder of the house designated this room for the infants of the family.

The floor plan was carefully laid out with the bathroom placed between the two rooms, to give the parents the privacy they needed and yet by keeping both doors opened, they could hear the infant's cries.

She wanted this room to be filled with joy and happiness of a baby. She knew that Thorton's abstinence of marital intimacy dashed all those hope.

She wanted a baby and she knew from her romance novels she needed Thorton to give her one.

'Yes, she would talk to him tonight.'

She stood still, looked around to see where she would start when she heard the door to the bathroom open and close, then the click of the lock.

She moved swiftly and quietly to the door leading to the bathroom. Because the previous family had so many children, the door remained open most of the time causing the door to warp slightly.

The slight warp caused a sliver of open space between the door and the frame. This small opening provided a clear view of the bathroom that contained the sink and the commode.

Thorton was standing with his back to her. He removed his pants and his under shorts. He was naked from his waist down.

He turned around.

Hatty clasped her hands over her mouth. The appendage between his legs was not the small limpid piece of flesh she saw on her wedding night but a large tumescent organ.

He cupped his hand around it and began to caress it. His movements were slow and gentle. He sat down on the commode, closed his eyes and smiled.

The swollen flesh grew harder and larger. He lowered his face between his legs and placed the swollen appendage in his mouth.

Hatty's eyes rolled as she fell into a deep faint into a heap of pillows at her feet.

When she came to, Thorton was gone. Now she knew, although she couldn't understand why, her husband would never give her the love, romance and children she wanted and needed.

The commode scene, as Hatty referred to it, Mentally flashed through her mind over and over. Shock, fear and repulsion consumed her.

She was now, more than ever, afraid of him. The confusion within the innocent, naïve girl took its toll. She spent most of her time in her bedroom reading with tears falling freely down her cheeks.

It was the arrival of Violet that changed the course of her life and thinking. Each day a tiny portion of her timidity vanished and an aggressive remark or act took its place. She had someone to love now and she would fight for it with a tenacity that sometimes frightened her.

Chapter Four

The legalization of Violet as Livinia Elizabeth Gilbert remained just that. Hatty referred to the child as Violet despite the many sharp reprimands by her husband.

She fought for the child's rights whenever she thought it necessary.

Her mother viewed this relationship with a cold, disapproving attitude.

"Stop wasting all your time on this child borne of sin, "She would retort. "What you need is a child of your own. A child borne of good breeding and a good, solid home."

Hatty would neither answer or defend herself. It didn't matter anymore what her mother thought. The child had brought sunshine into her life.

Going through the mail delivery one morning she found a letter addressed to her. That was unusual. No one ever wrote to her. It was from a Women's Private Clinic.

The message read:

Dear Mrs. Gilbert; Your mother Mrs. Rebecca Holwell requested an appointment for you with Dr. Attwater who will give you a through examination to determine the cause of your failure to bear children. Dr. Attwater is a renowned specialist in the field of gynecology with patients from every corner of the state. Your problem will be given the most knowledgeable analysis and evaluation known to medicine and will insure a positive solution to you problem. Your appointment has been set for Tuesday, May 24th at 2 P.M.

Hands trembling, Hatty had to sit down to temper her rage and fear.

'That woman,' As she referred to her mother who was still trying to run her life.

Her first impulse was to ignore the letter but knowing her mother she knew that this would not work. Furthermore she knew that her mother would be present to be informed of every detail.

Would the doctor know, she feared, there was nothing wrong with her? What could she say to him? What would he ask her? What should she do? What could she do to discourage her mother from being there?

Her life with Thorton flashed before her eyes. She saw herself in a dark, empty cave with her husband, in all his golden aura, blocking her exit.

She suddenly realized she had lived in that cave too long and it was about time she got out.

The appointment was two weeks away. That would give her time to plan her course of action. She was still sitting in the chair when Violet entered the room.

Violet was six years old now and no longer the frightened and confused little girl. She held out her shoe, "Look Auntie, the buckle on my shoe is broken."

Hatty looked down at the broken buckle and a thought flashed through her mind. "How would you like to go to the city for new shoes?"

"Oh yes," The child replied gleefully, "And a chocolate fudge Sundae at the soda shoppe."

Hatty grinned slyly, "Yes, shoes, ice cream and a new game we're going to play. It's a secret only you and I will share."

The trolley ride was a pleasant one for the two females, or the girls, as they were called. Violet sat on her knees, face pressed against the window. Hatty sat quietly piecing her plan into a neat picture.

She bought Violet her shoes, then went to the soda Shoppe for ice cream. After their repast they went to Woolworth and bought crayons and a coloring book.

Turning to the child, she whispered conspiratorially, "Now we are going to play our secret game."

Violet laughed quietly and whispered back, "What do I have to do?"

"I'll tell you when we get there," Hatty whispered back.

The child smiled happily.

Playing games had become part of their life. When Thorton was around they were quiet and well behaved. But when Thorton was out they were like two inmates just released from jail.

Hatty would sit down at the baby grand piano and play all the popular tunes of the day…jazz, blues, ragtime, unlike the somber church music Hatty was forced to play to entertain their guests.

They even went to the picture shows. Oh what fun they had and Violet thrived becoming more beautiful and loving with each passing day.

"Do you have an appointment?" The bobbed-haired, painted faced receptionist asked haughtily.

"Yes," Hatty smiled. 2 P.M. My name is Hatty Gilbert.

The girl looked down at her appointment book, looked up puzzled and returned her eyes to the book.

"I'm sorry but you must be mistaken. I have nothing here for a Mrs. Gilbert on May 4th."

Hatty took the letter out of her purse and showed it quickly to the girl. "Today is May 4th, isn't it? " Her heart pounding, she was counting on the hope that the girl wouldn't see the erasure of the '2' from the date.

"Yes, today is May 4th, but…"

Hatty looked at the girl questioningly. "My mother, Mrs. Rebecca Holwell made the appointment for me. I came to town today especially to see the doctor."

"Oh, Mrs. Gilbert," The girl gushed, "I'm so sorry for the error. I'll see if the doctor will see you. Please take a seat."

Hatty sat down triumphantly. So far her plan was working but her heart was still beating like drum.

She turned to Violet and whispered, "Honey we're playing our secret game now. You pretend you're coloring your book but you will be listening to everything that girl says."

"Yes, Auntie," Violet whispered back. Hatty winked at her slyly. The little girl winked back.

The door to the doctor's office opened and the receptionist said, "The doctor will see you now."

"Thank you," Hatty replied bravely and walked into the second part of her game.

A crisply dressed nurse took her into a room and handed her a white hospital gown, "Please undress and put this on. The doctor will be in shortly."

After the nurse left the room, Hatty placed the gown on the examination table and sat down. She had no intention of taking her clothes off.

She waited for the doctor hoping her courage would not fail her. She was listening to hard thumping of her heart when the door opened and Dr. Attwater entered.

Hatty's surprise was vocal and unintentional. The doctor was not at all what she expected-a kindly old man who treated everyone like his grandchild-but a woman. A beautiful, handsome woman.

"A woman doctor?"

Dr. Attwater smiled, "Surprised?"

"Yes," Hatty replied sheepishly, "I didn't think they allowed women to become doctors."

"I don't know what they are," The woman laughed, "But they didn't keep me from doing what I set out to do. Now tell me why you are still wearing your street clothes."

Hatty hesitated. Her plan had taken a slight twist but the friendly woman's smile instilled the courage that had been rising and falling all day.

"Doctor, I have a confession to make," A look of despair crossed her face. The doctor took her by the arm and motioned her to a chair.

Hatty gulped and continue, "I duped your girl. I wanted to see the doctor alone, without my mother being present."

The doctor nodded.

"There's nothing wrong with me," Hatty stammered, "The reason I don't have any children of my own is because...because..."

"Don't be afraid, Mrs. Gilbert," The doctor interjected, "I'm a doctor and whatever you say here will be in strict confidence."

The doctor wondered what secret this pretty, healthy looking girl was harboring.

"The reason is," Hatty kept her eyes down, "My husband and I...me...we don't , I guess you know what I mean."

"You mean you and your husband don't have sex?" The doctor asked bluntly.

"Yes, I mean no, we don't." Tears started to fall down her cheek as she twisted the gold wedding band on her finger.

Dr. Attwater gently picked up Hatty's chin, "Why?"

"Doctor," Hatty's anguished face looked up at the woman, "I'm not very wise in these matters. Anything I know is what I read in my romance novels."

"Which isn't much," The doctor retorted.

Hatty's confidence took a strong turn. "I want to tell you something," Her voice hesitated, "that is so dreadful I'm too ashamed to tell you but I have to know what it's all about."

She lowered her eyes again. Her voice fell to a mere whisper. "I feel it's all my fault"

"I doubt it," The woman reassured her, "But go ahead and tell me. Don't be ashamed. Perhaps it's not all that terrible and not your fault at all."

Hatty smiled gratefully and hesitantly went into a detailed account of the incident in the bathroom.

When she was finished she was trembling with shame.

The doctor took both of her hands into her own.

"My dear you're much too young and innocent and completely unaware about male and female relationships. Life is very complicated. Your husband doesn't have sex with you, not because of you personally but because you are a woman."

Hatty didn't know what the doctor was talking about. "He doesn't want to have sex with me because I'm a woman?"

"I hate to say this," Dr. Attwater continued, " Your husband will only have sex with men."

Hatty stared at her with her mouth agape. "With men?"

"Yes, men," The doctor emphasized the word men, "He's what is called in medical terms, a homosexual."

Hatty felt sick to her stomach. "I don't understand," She whispered through dry lips.

"My dear child," Dr. Attwater held tightly to Hatty's hands. "Your husband likes men. He will never seek or enjoy sex with any woman."

"But, but, "Hatty stammered, "Why did her marry me? And what was he doing in the bathroom?"

The doctor hesitated. This truly young, naïve, totally innocent young woman was being jolted by the sordid facts of life. She better give it to her straight. Pull no punches. She might as well learn the facts of life fast.

"Let's take one question at a time," The doctor spoke gently. "He married you because you are a pushover. He counted on your innocence and shyness and your total obedience, which he recognized immediately, to your parents and the church."

The doctor took a deep breath. "Second question...he was masturbating, or to put it in laymen's terms, he was playing with himself."

Hatty's face went white.

"He was having sex with himself," The doctor continued, "Because he didn't want a partner or he couldn't get one."

Hatty more confused and mystified whispered, "What shall I do?"

The doctor shrugged her shoulders, "Divorce him."

"I can't do that," Hatty gasped in horror, "We are very religious people."

Surprised, the doctor replied, "Don't religious people believe in sex?"

"Of course they do," Hatty became defensive.

The doctor patted her head, "Then get yourself a lover."

"Me?" Hatty drew back horrified.

"Yes you," Dr. Attwater answered matter of-factually. "If you don't you will continue living a dry, unfulfilled life. You need the love and affection of a man."

Hatty blushed furiously.

"I can see," The doctor continued, "That you are by nature a very sensuous woman and sensuous women need loving, sexually active men."

The color in Hatty's face grew brighter. Words stuck in her throat. "Where...where will I find this lover?"

The doctor smiled. "My dear just keep your options opened. You'll know who the right person is when he comes along."

Tears came to Hatty's eyes.

"Please," Continued the doctor, "Don't fill yourself with shame and guilt. God didn't create you to live a dry, barren life because he gave you a warm, sensuous body."

Smiling broadly, the doctor lowered her voice conspiratorially, "There's a great revolution going on in the world of women. One day it's going to explode into a national and world wide movement."

Hatty didn't know what the woman was talking about.

The doctor put her hand on the tearful Hatty, "Please keep in touch, you need someone to confide in. I'm into the quiet revolution and I'll do everything I can to help you be the whole person you deserve to be."

Hatty left the office troubled yet excited.

On the trolley ride back she lost herself in deep thought. Violet had to gently poke her now and then to get her attention.

'A lover,' She mused, 'Oh how marvelous it would be to have a strong pair of arms to rest her weary head. Warm and passionate kisses to light the fires smoldering under the surface of her skin.

'Yes,' she smiled, 'I'll find myself a lover, a beautiful, sexually exciting one just like the ones in my novels.'

Then a terrible thought crossed her mind, 'Where will I find him? I don't go anywhere. The only men I meet are the staid, rigid clergy Thorton brings home to dinner.

She was quietly tossing these questions and answers when the click and clang of the trolley beat a tempo into her consciousness and her mind kept repeating, 'Seek and ye shall find; Seek and ye shall find.'

Hatty laughed out loud. Violet turned and saw a happy, blushing woman with stars in her eyes.

For weeks Dr. Attwater's words danced inside Hatty's head with the electricity and excitement of a loop ride in a carnival. Up and down went her thoughts, around twists and turns then slowing down to a glide.

'How,' she thought,'Does one go about getting a lover?' Her life was wrapped up in her home and the care of Violet. There was no room for thrills and excitement in the home of the Reverend Thorton Gilbert.'

His preaching was mushrooming into a successful business venture. This brought more demands on Hatty to play the hostess to visiting ministers, church administrations and lately some state-wide political figures. Thorton was playing the field.

She played her part well. As the daughter of a minister who grew up in this social atmosphere and accepted her obligations naturally.

She could not, in all her fantasies, see a potential lover among the men Thorton brought home.

'No matter,' Hatty told herself, 'I'll look in every possible place I can think of.'

In her quest she began taking trips to town on any pretense.

Violet loved these excursions. Sometimes they went to the Theatre to see Vaudeville or to a moving picture show where exciting happened on a big white sheet while a man played the piano.

They always had lunch in the most crowded restaurants. The more crowded it was the better she liked it. She did not seek out the quiet, refined places where supposedly the best people went.

Each day a bit of the old, repressed Hatty disappeared and a newer, bolder, more daring Hatty emerged.

She took Violet to carnivals, to concerts in the park and even to a rodeo.

The sight of handsome, virile men riding their horses sent Hatty's head spinning. These men were part of her fantasy.

Life was becoming a merry-go-round and this once, shy girl did not want to get off.

Thorton didn't notice any changes because Hatty and Violet played their little game of obedience very well.

Downtown was lively with shoppers. It had been a fun day for Hatty and Violet. The little girl was skipping and practically dancing on her toes as the two walked to the trolley stop.

"I just remembered," Hatty exclaimed, "I forgot to buy myself a bonnet."

Violet ever ready to continue the fun, chirped, "Let's go back Auntie, I'm not tired."

"But I am," Replied Hatty, "Another time sweetheart."

"Look," Shouted Violet, "Across the street, over there."

The little girl pointed to a shop whose awning read, 'The Hat Shoppe.'

Violet was learning to read and she loved trying to read each and every sign she saw.

'That's strange,' Thought Hatty, 'I've never seen that shop before. It must have just opened.'

They crossed the street and peered into the shop. It's mullioned bay window, richly draped, displayed an ornate bombe chest. On it was a softly brimmed black straw hat resting lightly on crushed periwinkle blue colored crushed silk fabric.

The top draw was slightly opened and scarves of different shades of blue cascaded down its side.

Hatty and Violet entered. Inside , the shop was elegantly furnished and fragranced with perfume.

Soft, rose silk fabric covered the walls and an Aubusson rug graced the highly polished wood floor. Furnished to look like a drawing room, there was a moss green petit point sofa, two matching slipper chairs and several tables with glass globe lamps throwing soft light into the room. A cheval mirror placed against one wall gave a hint as to the room's purpose.

Hatty was taken back by all this opulence, thinking it was too rich for purse, she turned to leave.

The heavy rose colored drapery separating the shop from the back room, parted.

Hatty stopped short. An astonished look crossed her face.

Standing before her was her mother's former maid. The Irish girl with the fiery red hair, was now smartly dressed in a gray silk chemise with the hemline above her knees. Her hair, cut into a short bob, allowed her curls to run riot all over her head.

"Mimi?" Hatty asked in astonishment.

"Hatty," Beamed Mimi as she opened her arms in greeting. They embraced warmly laughing like two school girls.

The last time they saw each other was on the morning of Hatty's wedding day. Mimi brought her a breakfast tray.

"This is so special, lassie. "I'm going against your mother's wishes and bringing you a bit of food and pampering."

"Oh, thank you," The nervous bride-to-be murmured.

The girl sat the tray on the writing desk, drew up a chair and gently sat Hatty down.

"I brought you tea and biscuits with butter and jam. Nothing heavy to upset you but enough to keep you from falling flat on your face."

Hatty took a sip of tea.

"Now listen to me lassie," the girl whispered in her soft lilt, "You're an innocent creature, you are, and you are surrounded by powerful men who will never understand you, therefore you'll need a female to talk to every now and then."

Hatty put her cup down and looked strangely at the carrot top girl.

Mimi continued, "There are things you can never discuss with your mother. So, if you ever need someone to talk to, don't hesitate to come to me."

Hatty in her nervous state, couldn't understand what the girl meant. 'Talk? Talk about what? What was there to talk about?

There was a genuine warmth in the maid's offer and the bride-to-be smiled and numbly thanked her.

Shortly after she heard her mother had dismissed the Irish girl from her employ stating she was too Catholic for the Holwell household. Her constant crossing herself irritated Mrs. Holwell.

That was four years ago. Now the Irish immigrant maid was standing among all this elegance looking glamorous and very rich.

Mimi noticing a puzzled expression on Hatty's face, laughed uproariously. It's all mine, lassie. A very good friend made it possible for me to get a bank loan."

"I'm so happy for you," Hatty smiled brightly, "I just know you will be very successful."

"That's for sure, lassie, that's for sure. Now can I interest you in a bonnet."

"That's why we came," Violet chimed in, "Auntie needs a new hat."

Mimi brought out some hats and scrutinized Hatty. "Lassie, I think you need a fashion overhauling."

"I need what?" Hatty queried surveying herself in the mirror.

"Lassie, you are a very pretty girl but you are burying that beauty in drab, unflattering clothes."

Hatty became defensive. "You forget my husband is a preacher. I must dress the part."

Mimi took her by the shoulders and faced her, "That's all the more reason you should dress up. Your husband is becoming more famous with each passing day. And why should you dress fashionably? Because your husband is flamboyant. He dresses to kill. He uses his body and his voice to mesmerize silly women with his blood and thunder sermons."

Hatty looked at Mimi in disbelief. She was taken back by Mimi's harsh words. She had started to defend him then thought it better to let Mimi talk. Perhaps the girl knew a great deal and would be willing to talk about it.

"How am I supposed to dress?" Hatty puzzled.

"Leave it to me," Mimi smiled brightly, "When I get through with you, that handsome husband of yours will look at you through different eyes and start treating you like a real woman."

'What was Mimi talking about? What did she know? Did her mother know? What about her brother?'

Her mind was whirling with these thoughts when Violet tugged at her sleeve.

"Auntie, Mimi is beautiful and she's going to make you beautiful too. Won't that be nice? Then Uncle Thorton won't be so mean to you."

Hatty reeled, "Uncle Thorton isn't mean to me."

"Oh yes he is," Violet cried, "My daddy and mommy hugged and kissed all the time. They went to bed together and laughed and played. You sleep alone at night?"

Hatty's heart almost stopped beating. 'What was this child saying? How did she know how Thorton was really treating he? This child remembered a happy time with her parents and was comparing her and Thorton's life style with theirs.

Panic filled her. Then rage.

She turned to Mimi, "Go ahead, dress me."

Besides hats, Mimi carried a whole selection of high fashion dresses, shoes and accessories, none of which were on display to the public. This shop catered to a very special clientele.

She selected a whole new wardrobe for Hatty which transformed the drab, almost invisible girl, into a blooming flower.

On the way to the trolley stop, Hatty, excited and thrilled, her mind dancing with visions of men swooning at her feet, never noticed her brother Joshua entering the shop.

Chapter Five

Baptized Dominique Mc Clure, Mimi was raised on the bleak island of Aran, off the windswept Atlantic coast of Ireland.

The tenth child in a family of thirteen, Mimi's life was as bleak as the hard scrabble land that was her home.

All the Mc Clure children, except Mimi, inherited the dark hair and coloring of the silkies, a folk lore myth that claimed seals turned into humans when they came ashore looking for their mates.

Blazing red hair and suede gray eyes, Mimi was a presence on that island that could not be ignored.

She was a cardinal in a family of blackbirds.

"Are you sure she is not a creature from the depths of hell?" Locals would ask her tired and overworked parents.

Even her father would look at her with suspicion but he loved this child and knew she was his because she inherited his countenance.

The Priest told him that God willed it so because somewhere in his ancestry there was a red-headed viking who had set foot on the island and left his mark.

"You can tell," The Priest stated, "She has the bearing of a leader."

"God gave her to us to embarrass us," The mother would wail and hug the child at the same time.

All of this somehow escaped Mimi, she had a strong spirit and wisdom beyond her years. She knew she was destined for something other than living on this bleak island.

As soon as the children in the Mc Clure family grew up they were put into domestic service in the cities of Ireland.

There was no room for them in the tiny Mc Clure cottage. They left willingly and gladly.

Mimi loved the wild, rough sea outside her door. She would help her father tend to his fishing nets and he in turn regaled her with stories and fairy tales.

She worried that her father would never come back from his fishing trips and prayed hard for his return.

"It's God's will," Her mother would say if the sea swallows him up. He's a silkie and he will have returned home."

Mimi couldn't except that premise and doubled her prayers.

Her prayers were always answered. He did come home every night from the lashing wild seas but she lost him to an overworked heart after an exceptionally rough storm.

He brought his boat back to the quay, handed over his catch to the Co-Op agency and collapsed.

Shortly after, her mother announced she was leaving the island to go live with her sister in Dublin and made arrangements to send Mimi to America.

Mimi was intrigued by America. It's bigness, it's hustle and bustle and mostly it's multi-cultural population. America in turn was intrigued with Mimi, especially the men.

At first it was pleasant having all this attention and flattery tossed at her, then it started to turn ugly.

Her cousin's husband saw a gold mine in this big, beautiful red head and decided to earn money from her charms.

Mimi had had a warm and loving relationship with her father and adored men for their strength, protection and romantic natures and was looking for someone with those qualities.

She flatly refused her cousin's husband's proposal.

Realizing her life was in danger, Mimi kissed her cousin goodbye and went directly to the job agencies that dotted the New York waterfront.

These agencies were the starting point for the multitude of immigrants. Here there were job offers from all over the country.

"How far away is Kansas form New York City?" Mimi inquired after reading a list of jobs for men to work on the railroads and women as domestics.

"Far," The clerk announced, "It's called the prairie. Lots of land. Lots of opportunities. They need domestics if you're interested."

"I'm interested," Mimi replied quickly, "How do I get there?"

"By train," The clerk smiled, "And the fare will come out of your wages."

Mimi arrived in Kansas and promptly began working in the Holwell household.

She loved the big Victorian house with the gleaming woodwork, the expensive rugs, the beautiful lamps that threw off soft lights.

This was heaven to the impoverished Mimi. She even loved her bedroom under the eves in the attic.

The single size bed with a table and lamp beside it plus the dresser for her clothes was in deep contrast to the cot in the corner of her parents cottage where privacy was unknown and the sharing of a bed with two cousins in New York City.

She would go to her room after a days work tending to the household chores and daydream of all the wonderful things that were going to happen to her.

She found the Reverend and Mrs. Holwell stern, cold and calculating but found great joy in Hatty and Joshua.

Joshua was happy and easy going. Hatty was so shy, she carried a frightened look about her and had a tendency to stutter.

Her heart went out to this pretty girl and befriended her in any way she could.

He heart also went out to Joshua but in a different way, a feeling of mixed emotions. He was a happy, friendly person who was trapped in the strange world of religion she had trouble comprehending.

The house was always filled with visitors but there was never any laughter. There was never any joyous noise in this house but she still loved being there because she loved the surroundings and the two young people in it.

Chapter Six

The following day after Hatty and Violet's trip to the hat shoppe , Joshua called and announced he was passing through town and would like to spend the night at the Gilbert house.

Thorton was out of town and Hatty joyously looked forward to a pleasant visit without Thorton dominating the scene.

"Come Violet," Hatty sang, "My brother Josh is coming to visit."

The little girl caught in the glow that surrounded Hatty, followed her around the house while she cleaned and straightened furniture and bric-a-brac that was already cleaned and straightened.

Hatty smiled at the little girl, "Why don't you take a nap. You'll be fresh and rested when Uncle Josh gets here."

Violet loved her big poster bed where she would sink down into the lamb's wool mattress and dream of the soft tropical nights of another life.

Lying on the soft cloud she would hear her mother's soft, lilting voice in accented English singing. The voice floated down to the little girl in the words of her favorite lullaby…'I love my little baby, I love my little girl, she gives me lots of pleasure, she's my very own treasure.'

Violet would glance at the framed picture of the pretty woman, who was almost a child herself, and a smile would caress the child's face.

Soon the soft, rhythmic breathing of sleep whispered through the room.

By four o'clock the house fragrant with the sweet smell of baking and the mouth-watering aroma of a maple syrup glazed ham.

The table was set with fine bone china and gleaming sterling silver. A centerpiece of fresh flowers and candles floated in water in a shallow, lead crystal cut-bowl.

Hatty never put flowers on the table when she dined alone with her husband. It was one of the subtle rejections in her relationship with him.

She was putting the finishing touches to a lemon pudding when Joshua arrived. She flew into his arms and joyously embraced him.

Joshua was a tall, slender man, in contrast to his smallish, rounded sister. But they had the same face which was pretty on her and stunning on him.

His face was his fortune. It kept his adversaries off guard. He was gaining a reputation as one of the best tax lawyers in the mid-west.

They were finishing their dessert when he looked around and smiled sheepishly at Hatty and Violet. "What would you girls like me to bring back from Switzerland?"

"Switzerland?" Shrieked Hatty.

"Yes, Switzerland, "Replied Joshua.

Violet put the dessert spoon down and closed her eyes. Joshua's words faded into a soft, musical, accented voice.

'Violet my darling, when we get to Switzerland, everything will be fine.'

Joshua's voice came back through the haze of time.

"We're going to Switzerland to set up our world banking headquarters there."

"But why Switzerland?" Hatty asked.

"It's the safest place to keep money," Joshua replied, "The Shepherds Followers can conduct their European business expeditiously and safely. People from all over the world keep Swiss accounts for safety."

Joshua's voice faded again and the soft, musical voice took it's place.

'It's a safe place honey. In Switzerland our future will be assured.'

Hatty's voice broke through the haze. "Is it legal for an average American to have a Swiss account?"

It's legal. Many Americans have their money in Swiss accounts just for the privacy. It's called private money. Only you and the Swiss bank know about it. No one can check into these accounts because they are protected by the Swiss Government."

Hatty's face took on a serious overtone. "Can I have a Swiss bank account?"

Joshua's brow furrowed, "Why would you want one?"

Hatty hestitated, "Well, I...I'm sure you're aware of the situation in this household."

"I'm more than aware," Joshua growled. As the tax attorney for the Shepherds Followers he had his suspicions of Thorton. He didn't like the cold, ambitious preacher. He didn't trust him. He was always disturbed by Thorton's attitude towards Hatty. No man had the right to interfere between a husband wife but it was difficult to keep a neutral attitude towards the relationship.

Hatty folded her napkin into a quartered handkerchief pattern, "I have some money."

"Oh?" A surprised look crossed Joshua's features.

"I scraped it off every account in this household." She fumbled with the napkin. I want you to put it in a Swiss bank account for safety and privacy."

Joshua's face registered total disbelief. He was too stunned to talk. Suddenly he howled with laughter.

"Why you foxy little creature. I was so worried about you. I always took you for little Miss Innocent."

Hatty smiled broadly, "You mean little Miss Stupid. I'm not as dumb as I look, or timid anymore. I know how to play a few games too."

"I can see that," Joshua laughed.

Hatty became serious again, "I don't care about myself, Josh, I do care about Violet. She has been my salvation in this intolerable household."

Hatty's voice faded and the soft, musical voice drifted in, 'We're living dangerously, my little darling and this money is our salvation.'

The voice drifted away.

Hatty and her brother were so caught up in this new revelation they did not notice Violet slide out of her chair and leave the room.

The two adults were still laughing when Violet returned. In her hands was the ivory framed photograph of her parents.

She went to Hatty and handed her the photo. Hatty stopped laughing. "Sweetie is anything wrong?"

Violet pointed to the frame, "Open it, open it."

Hatty looked at her brother. He was staring at the intricately carved ivory frame.

Hatty was puzzled. She turned to the child, turned back to her brother, then back at the child.

"Open what, Violet?"

The child thrust the frame into Hatty's hands, pointed to the frame and excitingly said, "Open it, Auntie, Switzerland."

Hatty looked at her brother. A look of recognition lighted his face. "Hatty have you ever examined this frame?"

"No," Hatty replied dumb founded, "She would never let me touch it."

She held the frame in her hands, "I don't see anything unusual other than the intricate carvings."

"Look closely," Joshua urged, "I think Violet's been harboring a secret."

"A secret?," Hatty repeated, "What kind of secret?"

Joshua took the frame and examined it. Violet went over to him and pointed to a spot on the frame.

"Push," She commanded.

Joshua pushed at the spot but nothing happened.

"Up," Violet jumped up and down, "Up."

Joshua pushed down on the spot again then up.

"Like this?" He asked.

"Yes," She clapped her hands with delight. "Now push hard."

Joshua pushed harder. Suddenly the frame began to come apart.

Hatty and Joshua gasped with astonishment and the child clapped her hands in glee as the hollowed ivory frame revealed fifty, one –thousand dollar bills.

Brother and sister looked at the money in disbelief. "Well I'll be damned," An awed Joshua exclaimed.

"Switzerland," Sang Violet holding some of the bills. "Safe, Maman said go to Switzerland. Take it Uncle Josh, take it to Switzerland."

Joshua picked up the child and sat her on his lap, visibly shaken by the discovery.

"Violet honey, I think fate has decreed that we full fill your mother's wishes."

His voice faded and the soft musical voice drifted in, 'somehow, some way we will make it to Switzerland, you'll see.'

The voice drifted away and Joshua smiled down at Violet. Her gave her a bear hug and turning to his sister, he shook his head in wonderment and said, "Destiny is the choreographer of life."

Chapter Seven

I'm having some very important people over for dinner," Thorton announced one morning. Dinner will commence at seven."

It was not unusual for Thorton to invite guests and tell Hatty that same day. It seemed as if he was testing her to make some mistake so that he could demean her one more time.

"How important and whom might they be," She asked boldly.

"They are," Thorton replied emphatically, "The men behind the men who will be in the new administration in Washington after the election."

"Why are they so important to you?" Hatty continued her bold questioning.

He turned to her, his face bearing a sly smile, "Important enough for your father's deep displeasure if the evening is not successful."

She hated these dinners, she never knew what to talk about.

"I and your father would appreciate it if you join in the conversation once in a while instead of sitting there like a deaf mute."

Her boldness quickly deflated. She retreated to the sanctuary of the kitchen to sort out her mind.

The thought of her father's displeasure sent chills up her spine.

Her marriage to Thorton did not soften her father's attitude towards her. To him, she was a female who had to be kept in line at all times.

Church business was his life and everyone around him had to arrange their lives accordingly.

The Reverend Holwell embraced whole heartily Thorton's preaching which was drawing larger crowds which brought more money to the coffers.

The young preacher fit nicely into the Reverend's scheme of life. What the Reverend didn't know was that he fit Thorton's scheme of life even more. With the Reverend Holwell behind him his star shone brighter than ever, why else would he have entered this disastrous marriage to the Reverend's mousy daughter.

Despite their success, father and son-in-law treated Hatty with indifference. They expected her to carry out her role as a Minister's wife with dignity and without any complaints.

Hatty was trapped and she knew it.

The dining table glowed with sparkling Waterford crystal, sterling silver flatware and green bordered, gold rimmed Limoge china. A silver candelabrum graced each end of the table. A center piece of scented candles and gardenias completed the setting.

With the help of Gretchen, a German immigrant neighbor, who hired herself out as a cook, Hatty was able to accomplish her dinner party in time for the guests arrival. The cook's son acted as a butler.

Violet watched the preparations with the curiosity and anticipation of something magical to happen.

"Auntie, can I come to your party?" The sparkle in her smoky blue eyes lit up her face.

"It's 'may I ' honey and I'm afraid not," Hatty replied sadly, "But I'll show you how to play a game I played when my parents had company."

The child smiled gleefully, "What kind of game?"

Hatty took Violet by the hand and took her up the staircase and placed her behind a potted plant located at the top of the landing.

"You stay here, don't let anyone see you. From this position you can see all the visitors as they come in. After they enter the dinning room, go into the kitchen and Gretchen will give you a big piece of chocolate cake and a glass of milk. After you drink your milk go to your room and I'll come by later and tell you all about the party."

All right Auntie and I'll be very quiet behind the plant." The little girl and the woman hugged each other.

Hatty went down the stairs to await the arrival of her guests while the little girl hid behind the plant.

At precisely six thirty Thorton arrived with guests; two elderly men, friends of her father; her father and a young man, an easterner by his appearance and with the dark good looks of a southern European background.

The guests assembled in the parlor for an aperitif of mint julep tea. "This is my daughter Hatty," The Reverend Holwell said to the stranger. To Hatty he said "This is Settimus Adamo."

Hatty no longer looked at feet when she met strangers. She now held her head high. She saw a head full of dark unruly curls, no amount of brilliantine could tame.

His features were strong and foreign looking as if he stepped out of an ancient Roman history book.

Her eyes sought his and found herself looking into a pair of smoldering coal-black eyes.

Suddenly the words of Dr. Attwatter resounded in her head. Impulsively she extended her hand, a gesture she knew her father would disapprove of and in a strong voice said, "Pleased to meet you Mr. Adamo."

The stranger smiled, "Please call me Sonny," and took her hand. He held it gently but firmly, "It's indeed my pleasure to meet you Mrs. Gilbert and for allowing me the honor of dining with you this evening."

Thorton always sat at the head of the table with Hatty at his left. Not tonight. Before the guests entered the dining room Hatty changed the place cards and put herself at the other end, a place she should have always sat as the wife of the host.

She placed her father on Thorton's right and Mr. Adamo at her right. She informed the butler of the seating arrangement and at the stroke of seven sent him in to the parlor to announce dinner.

Thorton;s face showed extreme displeasure at the change in seating. Surprisingly her father looked pleased. Hatty gave the butler the signal to commence.

Thorton looked at his guests and they all bowed their heads in prayer. His voice, resonant and pious after reciting the Lord's prayer, went into a lengthy blessing.

Hatty with head still bowed, raised her eyes and glanced at Mr. Adamo. His head was upright, his eyes curiously on her.

She smiled. He smiled. She lowered her eyes and kept them down until her husband finished.

The Reverend Holwell opened the conversation . "Mr. Adamo, we want you to know that we appreciate your coming to Kansas and that we are all ready to help you, help us get Mr. Hoover nominated this June at the National Convention."

"We'll do everything possible," Thorton interjected, "To make your stay in Kansas as productive as possible."

"I'm sure you will," Settimus answered, "Putting a prohibitionist in the White House is important to the growth and safety of this nation." Everyone nodded their heads in agreement. "But I'm wondering if I might impose upon you a rather revolutionary idea to implement this campaign."

Reverend Holwell looked at the easterner with suspicion, "What do you mean by revolutionary?"

Settimus smiled broadly. "In the east we employ a large female staff. We found women to be a driving force in getting our men in office."

The men looked at him horrified.

Settimus laughed loudly. "You're shocked. But as a political consultant for successfully elected congressmen and governors, I can assure you I'm not speaking off the top of my head.."

He turned to Hatty, "Mrs. Gilbert, wouldn't you want to be part of the history of this great country?"

Hatty blushed furiously.

"Wouldn't you," continued Settimus, "Want the excitement of working in a campaign that will get Herbert Hoover, a great engineer and a Quaker, into the White House?"

All Hatty could think of was Settimus's eyes; smoldering, mysterious, seductive. What did she care who became President of the United States? Washington, D.C. was in another place, another world, another life. Mr. Hoover was not going to solve her problems-or was he?

Before she knew what was happening, the words flew out of her mouth, "Yes, I think I would, Son...Mr. Adamo,"

'Get hold of yourself', she thought, 'Something is happening here.'

Thorton laughed, "The idea of Hatty working with crowds of people is ridiculous. She is perpetually tongue-tied."

Hatty gave her husband a dark, angry look. She turned to Settimus and strongly announced "I would very much like to work and help you in this campaign."

She looked to Thorton again, this time smiling, "I'm sure my husband will be very pleased." Hatty's breath caught in her throat.

None of her husband's guests ever gave her more than a passing nod. For that matter they hardly noticed her. Now all eyes were upon her.

She was enmeshed in the ecstasy of the moment when her father's voice cut into her, "Don't you have things to attend to in the parlor for our after-dinner coffee?"

Her moment of happiness turned into rage. Boldly she answered back as she had never done before in her life, "Everything as been taken care of, Father, including the Havana cigars you seem to like so much."

The Reverend backed up a little at his mousy daughter's impertinence but before he had a chance to respond she turned back to this handsome easterner, "Mr. Adamo," She smiled, "What would Mr. Hoover's being president do for our country?"

He laughed, "For one he is a Quaker and he will keep prohibition, an effective law against drinking, alive and well."

Hatty smiled broadly.

"Don't be fooled," He continued, "By my New York look and speech, I'm very much against liquor. It destroys lives."

She smiled coquettishly, "On the contrary, although your New York looks and speech will not go unnoticed, we know there are many people all over the country who agree with us, including the New York population."

She smiled at her guests, excused herself and went into the hall to the bottom of the staircase. She looked to see if Violet was still behind the potted plant.

The little girl knew how to play the game well. "Violet," Hatty's called softly, her voice barely above a whisper.

Violet's face peered between the posts. "What is it, Auntie?" Her voice matching Hatty's in timbre. "Keep your ears and eyes wide open. I want to know everything they say when they come out into the hall."

"Yes, Auntie, I'll listen very carefully."

"Good, I'll see you in a little while to tuck you in."

"I want to show you something," Violet giggled later as Hatty was tucking her under the covers. She opened the palms of her hands and produced a ten-dollar bill.

"Where did you get that," Hatty gasped.

"Sonny gave it to me."

"Sonny? You mean Mr. Adamo?"

"I guess so. He told me to call him Sonny."

"When did he tell you that?" Hatty's heart was starting to race.

When he came out in the hallway. He said, "Hi ya beautiful, what are you doing?"

Violet giggled again. "I told him I was keeping my ears and eyes wide open for Auntie Hatty and to tell you everything that happened."

"Hatty was horrified. "What did he say then?"

Violet's eyes twinkled. "He said I was as beautiful as you and to keep up the good work. Then he gave me the money and told me to treat you to a chocolate fudge sundae."

Later that night too charged up to sleep, Hatty was in bed with a book when the door flew open.

Thorton loomed in the doorway, his face purple with rage.

"How dare you agree to work with that New York wop."

Hatty's mouth opened in disbelief, "How dare you," He continued to fume, "Humiliate me in front of my colleagues, not to mention your own father."

Hatty's reaction was terror but this pious man who preached the humility of Jesus, committed a deadly sin by resorting to vile bigotry, rubbed raw on her nerves.

Courage that was coming to her in small doses, now exploded into one big mega dose.

She quickly got out of bed and stood there glaring at him. Then in a calm voice she said, "If you call that humiliation, then you haven't see anything yet that measures up to it if I tell the world that our marriage has never been consummated because you are a homosexual."

"Also you do terrible things to yourself in the bathroom."

Thorton froze.

"How long did you think," She continued in the same calm voice, "That I was going to remain the shy, naïve-not stupid-but naïve girl I was when you married me to further your ambitions?"

Thorton stared at her in disbelief.

Her head and shoulders rose so that she looked taller and more confident, "I confess when I first saw your wretched behavior in the bathroom I was frightened and confused but I made it my business to find out just what you were doing."

His mind reeled with terror but he composed himself and between clenched teeth hissed, "Do you think any one would believe you, the mouse that trembles."

He laughed wickedly.

"Perhaps," She smiled back, "But there will be an investigation if I make a formal complaint."

His face went white. "I won't let you do this terrible thing to me."

"You can't stop me," She retorted, "No matter what terrible thing you plan, your career will be over. I am and always was your stairway to the stars."

Thorton collapsed into the chair and put his head in his hands.

She stood there looking down at him with as much hatred that a loving and romantic woman could muster. A million things crossed her mind.

Divorce? Her father had the capacity make her the aggressor and this pitiful man the victim. Thorton was the money maker. She was irrelevant.

Scandal? Never. She would be sent away to some camp in the desert and become a prisoner for life.

Confusion began to seep in but this quickly passed as anger took over. This was not the way her life was supposed to be. Fate played a dirty trick on her. There never was, and never will be a shinning knight on a white horse to sweep her off her feet and carry her off into the sunset.

There will never be a lover with strong, protective arms to shield her from life's hardships. No romance. No nights of tender passion. Nothing.

'Damn' she thought, 'If she couldn't have what was rightfully hers, she was going to replace it with something else.'

'What could possibly take the place of a loving man, a man she dreamed about all her life, to be by her side.'

Thorton remained in the chair, defeated by his weakness. His head still in his hands.

What a pitiful sight to behold, she reflected. A man who could sway crowds of people and hold them in the palms of his hands, was actually groveling at her feet.

Suddenly like a bolt of lightening, she knew what she was going to do, because now, she, the little mouse that trembled, was going to roar.

"If you want to be the rising star on the horizon." She announced, "Pick your head up and listen to what I have to say."

He picked up his head and listened. He didn't like what he heard but he had no choice, she held the winning card.

Chapter Eight

From that day on Hatty transformed, as if by sorcery, into an entirely different person.

She wore fashionable and daring clothes. Watched her diet which changed her slightly plump figure into a sensuousness where she was no longer invisible.

She liked her new self and strangely so did those around her.

Her mother, as expected, was horrified. But Hatty calmed her down by telling her that that was the way Thorton wanted her to dress. It complemented his image.

She also took Mr. Adamo's advice and went to the local campaign office to work for Hoover's election.

There she met a couple of women, mostly former suffragettes who were very vocal and aggressive and involved in anything that put them on a soap box.

At first she found them frightening but began to warm up to them when she realized they were very much their own persons who would not let anyone control them.

She found they were also liberally sexual and spoke freely about their encounters. Hatty listened carefully to everything they said. They became her role models and she began, slowly and carefully, to ask them questions.

She also began visiting the hat shop where Mimi's honesty and Irish wit made her laugh. She was still curious about Mimi's good fortune but kept her silence in order to keep the friendship.

And she dreamed of Sonny Adamo. His smoldering eyes so full of mystery marched in and out of her dreams. She saw herself melting into his arms. His strong New York accent adding to his attraction which conjured up a life full of excitement and glamour.

She replayed the night he came to dinner, remembering everything he said. The way he looked at her. The way she felt. She wondered where he was. She knew he was traveling around the state and was hoping he would come back soon.

One day he did.

She was tacking cardboard signs to carrying sticks when the distinctive New York accent broke into her thoughts.

Her heart stopped. Then began beating rapidly taking her breath away.

Smiling broadly, he took one of the signs and held it up, "You're doing a great job, Mrs. Gilbert."

Regaining her composure she smiled back, "Thank you Mr. Adamo. I took your advice and I'm finding campaigning very exciting and rewarding."

He took her arm, "How about rewarding me for my good advice by joining me in the dinner across the street for a cup of java."

Hatty was about to refuse when she thought, 'Why not,' "I'll be delighted to join you."

Sitting across from Sonny was an emotional roller coaster that sent her feelings into a tail spin.

At first she was embarrassed to be seen with a stranger but Sonny was able to put her at ease with his comedic stories about street life in New York City.

"Have you ever been to my city?" He asked looking intently at her over his coffee cup.

"Oh no," She smiled weakly, "I've never been out of the state except to Oklahoma over the state line."

"That's too bad," He replied, "New York needs a woman like you to bring some of your religion to that wicked place."

"Don't you have religion in New York?" Hatty asked innocently.

He laughed his slightly crooked smile that sent her heart spinning, "We have plenty of religion only it's preached by a bunch of old men."

Pointing at her, he said, "Now you would make those poor miserable souls sit up and take notice. There are a lot of deaf kids going unnoticed and untaught."

She was appalled, "Isn't anyone teaching these children?"

"Hardly," He sighed, "They need someone like you to start up a program for deaf kids. What do you say, are you willing go to New York and give it a try? I'll help you get started."

"What about Violet?" Hatty asked, "What will I do with her. I can't leave her here and go to New York."

"Bring her along. Come in the summer during school vacation. I have plenty of good people who will take care of her while you do your good work."

"I'll think about it," She replied sadly and almost to herself whispered, 'I want to go so badly.'

He raised his cup in a toast and smiled, "I'll make all the arrangements on my side while you make yours here. Just let me know and I'll take care of everything."

Hatty walked to the hat shop in a daze. Mimi stopped short, "Good Lord lasssie, did you walk into a trolley? Here sit down."

She accepted the seat and started to laugh then immediately went into a crying jag.

Mimi became alarmed. She put her arms around Hatty and rocked her in her arms. "It's alright lassie, I'm sure it's not that bad. You're all in one piece. I'll make you a cup of tea and you can tell me, if you want, what this is all about."

Hatty was settled down and while sipping her tea mumbled, "Oh Mimi, my life is so confusing."

Mimi eyed her critically. This poor creature, she thought , is being ripped apart by too many powerful people around her.

"Perhaps a good chat will clear your mind lassie."

Tears welled in Hatty's eyes. She took a hankie from her purse, wiped her eyes and gently blew her nose.

"Oh Mimi, I have to tell somebody or I will just explode."

The two women sat and chatted for some time. Hatty poured her heart out and told her friend the whole sordid story of her marriage, her ultimatum to Thorton and offer from Sonny Adamo.

Mimi listened intently to everything Hatty told her. Her keen observations of life came from being born into a big, poor family in a famine stricken country where traditions controlled everyone's life. It was the poverty of her environment and the stiflingly restrictions of her family life that were released when she came to America to start anew.

She emphasized with Hatty and saw herself in the other girl's position.

"Take your freedom from wherever it comes," She advised, "Don't be afraid to take a chance. You have every right to the love of a good man."

Hatty sniffled.

"Just because you're trapped in a loveless and unconsummated marriage doesn't mean you can't have love. Go to New York this summer but go to your lady doctor first and let her advise you on how to take care of yourself. You're entitled to enjoy the fruits of life wherever and whenever you can."

The two women were hugging each other when the door to the shop opened and Joshua walked in.

Hatty was startled to see her brother. "Josh what are you doing here?"

His surprise was as evident as hers but he quickly composed himself and grinned.

"I came to see Mimi."

Hatty looked from one to the other, a puzzled look on her face.

"Mimi and I are old friends," Josh said, "In fact we're very good friends."

"But," Hatty stammered, "Mother let her go a long time ago."

"Joshua laughed, "Mother let her go but I didn't and I'm glad you found her. Mimi is now part of our lives."

"But Mother," Hatty mumbled.

"Please Hatty," Mimi pleaded, "Try to understand."

"Understand? Understand what? Will someone please tell me what's going on?"

"Sit down Sis," Josh now serious, "Because of our circumstances, yours and mine, we cannot live out lives the way we want. We cannot choose our mates. We have to live according to the rules of the Followers. We were born, so to speak into slavery."

Hatty slumped into her chair, "You're a man Josh, you can move around and go anywhere without any trouble. I can't."

Joshua knelt down beside her, took her face in his hands, "Oh yes you can. That which put us into chains, ironically has given us the freedom to move around the world, all in the name of the Lord."

"Josh," Hatty uttered in horror, "That's a terrible thing to say."

"Perhaps," Joshua replied, "But it's the truth."

Hatty looked at her brother quizzically, "If that's the way we have to live then I will start by going to New York City and open up a school for the deaf. Mr. Adamo will make all the contacts for me."

Joshua was pacing around the room, stopped short when Hatty mentioned Mr. Adamo's name. "What do you know about him?" Her brother asked.

"He's a political consultant," Hatty replied.

"Oh really?" Her brother replied.

"Yes, He's here to help Hoover win the nomination."

"What else do you know about him? Her brother quizzed.

"Very little, but if he can help me start a school for deaf children that's good enough for me."

Her brother sat down and sighed. "Your life has been so empty and will remain so, therefore like myself, you have to find some happiness wherever you can. Go to New York. Just be careful and remember I'll always be there for you."

"What about you and Mimi?" Hatty asked, "Where is this relationship going?"

"We don't know," Joshua sighed, "But we're taking our happiness wherever and whenever we can."

Mimi went over to Hatty and put her arms around the bewildered girl, "Life has a habit of punching us in the face, lassie, and I'm fighting back, Your brother and I have accepted our position in life without shame or guilt. He got me the bank loan for my little business and the upstairs flat is our little love nest."

Hatty looked at her brother and Mimi, first with disbelief then slowly with admiration.

She laughed out loud, "If Mother could only see us now," and they joined her in laughter.

Chapter Nine

Joshua Holwell was the bright rising star in the Holwell household. At an early age he showed a strong aptitude in the field of numbers.

He could add, subtract six digit numbers instantly. He said he could see the numbers clearly in front of him almost as if the quotations were written on a blackboard.

The Reverend constantly called the young boy to verify columns of figures. As the boy grew he could tell if a church project was financially profitable or a loss.

His astute father decided the boy should go to law school specializing in international law. His father could see clearly which direction the ministry would go with this number genius in charge of finances.

Joshua agreed to this course in his life as he saw himself traveling to different parts of the world living a privileged and luxurious lifestyle. His happy-go-lucky nature was an asset that would carry him far and assure a successful career.

Everything was going in his favor except for an important personal aspect.

His parents had a girl waiting in the wings to be his bride.

Joshua wasn't ready to settle down, in what he termed, domestic fraud.

He convinced his parents that his work would take him away from home and he would have no time to devote to wife and family.

"These are sacrifices women make for their men," His mother stated primly.

"I'm not ready yet, Mother," He would announce smiling, "When I'm established and can hold my own, I'll think about it."

"Don't think too hard," His mother reprimanded, "It's your duty to start a family."

Joshua gave her a big smile and a bear hug.

"For appearances sake," She pleaded, but her handsome son was a master at manipulating her in his sunny, lovable way and they left him alone with occasional references to young women from good Christian families who would make him a good, obedient wife.

He loved women and would bed them whenever there was an opportunity but his heart was held tight by the immigrant Irish maid with the fiery, red hair.

The trouble was he wanted his career and Mimi and was going to have them both. They were his life.

His gift of figures and his grasp of international law made him an excellent tax lawyer.

His ability to shift money legally brought in large profits to the church coffers and this was what the ministry wanted and this was what Joshua wanted.

Everything!

He was also healthily lusty. His sexual encounters satisfied his physical needs but left him wanting and yearning.

It was when he met Mimi, a maid in his boyhood home, that his heart became involved. He knew from the first moment he laid eyes on her that she was going to be a very important part of his life.

Mimi also felt he strong electrical currents between them but knew she could never be his wife.

And so it came about when Mrs. Holwell detected the attraction between her son and the maid that she fired the girl.

Joshua would not let go and set Mimi up in business and they would consummate their love in the flat above the hat shop.

Ironically, mistresses were accepted among the men in the ministry but discretion was demanded and Joshua carried on his love affair without interference.

It was an ideal arrangement. He had his freedom and love life all wrapped up in one neat little package but to Mimi and Joshua their love had the passion and concern for each other that comes once in a lifetime...love without guilt or shame.

Chapter Ten

Hatty announced her decision to go to New York City for the summer to open up her school to Thorton one night as he was ready to ensconce himself in the study.

He gave her hard look then shrugged his shoulders, "Do whatever makes you happy."

Hatty went to Dr. Attwater for advice. She asked many questions and the doctor answered them bluntly and with honesty.

With Hoover's nomination out of the way, Hatty and Violet prepared to go to New York City for the summer.

Sonny Adamo made all the arrangements for the two females. A place to live in an apartment hotel. A governess for Violet and space in a loft building for Hatty's school.

A chauffeured limo picked them up at Grand Central Station and took them to the hotel.

Violet bounced all over the place with delight. "Auntie, Daddy and Mommy always stayed at hotels," Violet sang.

The apartment was filled with flowers and a big fruit basket with a note. 'For two of the most beautiful women in the world. Please join me for dinner tonight,' signed simply 'Sonny.'

Hatty and Violet dressed carefully. A limo picked them up and took them to the Plaza. Seated in a quiet corner, Sonny greeted the girls with warmth and all the charm he was capable of displaying in public.

Hatty knew where this relationship was going and she was not going to stop it. She was going to start enjoying her life as she never had before.

'How does one go about having a relationship with a man? Every time she looked at his handsome face her heart melted. She then remembered Dr. Attwater's advice, 'Let everything happen naturally.'

And that's what she did.

Live moved swiftly. She started her school with six children and before she knew it she had fifteen students in her class.

Violet in the meantime had the time of her life with the governess Sonny provided. A French woman who spoke with a cultured accent. Claudine, opened up a whole new world to the little girl, taking her to the zoo, to children's theatre, shopping and all the sights and sounds of the big city. They even had a hot dog from one of the colorful carts that dotted the city.

Sonny stopped by the school many times to see how she was doing and if she needed anything.

One day he smiled broadly, "Tonight you and I are going dancing." Violet is going to spend the night at Claudine's so that we can stay out all night."

Hatty laughed deliciously. Would tonight be the night she had been breathlessly waiting for all summer?"

One of the things she did on arrival was to replenish her wardrobe from the smart Madison Avenue shops.

For this night she chose a simple chemise dress in a supple soft creme silk. She gathered her long hair into a becoming knot at the nape of her neck and let the small tresses of curls run riot around her face contrasting the effect of softness against the chic smartness of her dress.

She was dazzling and she knew it.

Sonny arrived promptly at eight, smiling from ear to ear. He took one look at her and said, "Wow!"

He walked her over to mirror on the wall and whispered, "Look."

He was standing behind her and gazed at her eyes in the silvered image. "Close your eyes," He continued to whisper.

She closed her eyes, "Now open them." In the mirror she saw a pearl necklace in his hands. "Let me put them around your neck," He brushed her face with his lips.

Her heart raced as his hands touched her throat sending tingles down her spine. "There," He said, "These pearls were meant for you."

"You shouldn't have," She finally murmured, trying her best to compose herself.

He laughed, "Oh yes I should have and you will wear them now and forever. They are yours."

The pearls felt warm against her skin. "I can't accept them," She cried.

"You have to," He stated firmly, "They are a token of my deep affection for you. You," he emphasized, "Have touched my heart." He brushed her cheeks again with his lips, "You and I have met by chance and as some fools have said that 'Never the t'wain shall meet' were wrong because we did."

He turned her around and looked her in the eyes. "Our life styles will keep us apart but we must and should live for the moment," He took her face in his hands and kissed her gently on the lips.

They had dinner in a private alcove of an elegant east side town house restaurant.

Food she never imagined existed was served by a handsome looking waiter who resembled an Olympic athlete.

They began their meal with a soft, white wine. He smiled, "This came from one of the few bottles left in my private wine cellar when it was legal to have a wine cellar. I kept it for a very special occasion.

She smiled. Her heart was racing so fast the legality of the wine was of no concern at this time. Her body was on fire.

The meal progressed slowly. First they had a clear broth followed by what looked like pancakes heaped with caviar and sour cream. Then a tiny bird nesting in a pastry shell accompanied by baby carrots and slender stalks of asparagus. All this accompanied by glasses of the soft wine. She felt as if she were in another world.

They talked about her life and how Violet came to live with her, all the while avoiding any talk about Thorton, until he asked her point blankly, "What kind of a relationship do you have with your husband?"

She paled. The words refused to pass her lips. He took her hand, "You don't have to tell me. I know."

"Know what?" She asked with horror.

"I'm a good judge of people. I have to be in my business." Hatty held her breath. "Your husband," He continue, "Is what he is and you should not blame yourself. I know divorce is out of

73

question. Live your life the way it suits you but never, ever lose that softness. It has absolutely touched my heart."

Tears glistened in her eyes.

"Come," He took her arm, "I promised you we were going dancing tonight."

He led her to a small elevator which took them up to a private suite. Scented candles were burning everywhere, sending flickering lights into the many shadows of the sitting room and the bedroom beyond.

He went over to a Victrola and placed the needle on the record. Soft music filled the room. He took her into his arms and they danced slowly.

The touch of his hands and the warmth of his body relaxed all the tensions she had been feeling. She was back in her romance novels as the fires of passion began to build up within he.

He buried his face into her hair. She filled him with a soft gentleness he never felt before in his life. He felt as if he was holding a precious treasure. He wanted her badly but was afraid to crack the fragileness of her.

They moved around the floor slowly and as the passion began to surface they moved from the sitting room into the bedroom.

He knew she was inexperienced so he initiated the first move. He unbuttoned the back of her dress slowly, slid it off her body.

She in turn began to undress him as the heroines did in her novels. They moved in slow motion as they undressed each other.

He gently laid her on the bed and kissed her face, then her neck. His lips moved slowly to her breast gently flicking the hard nipples then suckling them with a passion he could not control.

"Take me," She whispered hoarsely.

He entered her slowly, the hot moistness of her making him throb madly and sending sensations all over his body.

She felt his heat and hardness, a hardness she always dreamed about, wrapped her arms around him and brought him closer to her.

They moved in rhythm, first slowly and passionately until they both arrived at an explosive climax.

They spent the rest of the night exploring each other, sipping wine and dancing to the soft music. This was a night that sent her soaring to heaven. A night she would treasure all her life.

The rest of the summer went by in a blur of dazzling happiness. The school became established. Violet, entranced with all the city had to offer, laughed and danced her days away.

Finally it was time to go home. A terrible sadness came over Hatty. Her blissful nights were coming to an end. How could she endure what lay before her. It was time to take stock of her life.

Sonny had to go his way and she had to go hers. On their last night together, they held on to each other knowing it was their last night of love.

"Promise me," Sonny begged, "That you will take care of your life and come to me whenever you can,"

And so they parted, two star-crossed lovers whose hearts and bodies will live thousands of miles apart.

Chapter Eleven

Thorton in the meantime went on his merry way, gathering popularity which each passing day.

Every so often Hatty would appear with him when she needed his help in opening up another school.

These appearances were very effective. As Thorton spoke for the needs of the children, Hatty would stand next to him and repeat everything in sign language.

They looked so wholesome together people would stand and cheer as they smiled and waved to the crowds.

Thorton and Hatty were civil to each other. She played the part of the dutiful wife and hostess with skill and care.

Thorton had his men friends, which he had the nerve to bring home and ensconce themselves in the study.

She didn't care. In a sense her life was now peaceful and serene. She no longer looked to her husband for his love, only his support which he gave her to keep her from destroying him.

Every so often Hatty and Violet would travel to New York to check up on the school and to see Sonny. She missed him on her last trip. No one seemed to know where he was. She seemed to have lost contact with him. She dreamed about him every night and knew that he would appear from wherever he was.

Violet was growing into a stunning beauty. Hatty did not restrain her from having friends, male or female and even encouraged her into a very social life, combined with her duties of a religious life.

Violet began learning the sign language at a very early age. She became adept at it. When she became a teen-ager, she spent her summers at camps for deaf children.

Hatty kept nothing back from Violet. She told her the real facts of life. She even sent her to Dr. Attwater where she received a detailed education in sex.

Violet was being primed for life because Hatty knew that this beautiful girl was destined to follow in her footsteps.

Life moved swiftly and quietly and when Violet was just eighteen, war clouds loomed over the horizon.

At precisely 1.15 P.M. December 7, 1941, Japan bombed Pearl Harbor and the lives of millions of Americans changed forever. Patriotism surged with fevered passion. Religious beliefs surfaced from hidden depths.

Families were torn apart and blood and tears were shed unashamedly.

It also brought people from all over the land, from all nationalities, races and backgrounds together. People whose paths would have never crossed were thrown together changing the social and economic structure of America.

The Followers moved quickly into action with their declaration that they were conscientious objectors.

Thorton beat the drums fast and furious. "We are the Shepherds followers," He declared, "Advocating peace and good will."

The rumble from Washington was negative and threatening.

Thorton in his skillful, manipulative way created a medical team in order to protect his tax-exempt status.

Hatty moved quickly when Thorton made her head of the overseas division.

Violet who was now eighteen, joined Hatty and a contingent of medics and set up headquarters in North Africa where the American forces were fighting.

Hatty and Violet went right into action working steadily and efficiently keeping the medics supplied with first-aid material, well-oiled and well-kept ambulances and high morale.

Aside from ministering to the sick and wounded, Hatty's piano playing and Violet's sweet angelic voice were put to heavy use.

They played and sang all the romantic ballads of the day; Bing Crosby's White Christmas; Don't Sit Under The Apple Tree With Anyone Else But Me; The White Cliffs Of Dover and the Andrews Sister's famous Bugle Boy.

They were such a hit they were called 'The two flowers of the desert.'

"You made the desert bloom for me," A soldier whispered to Violet just before he died.

She cried for him but thanked the Lord she brought him joy in the last moments of his life.

There were many such incidents which made Violet, a sheltered flower in a walled garden, mature and grow far beyond her years.

The North African conflict was over and a temporary peace perfumed the air. Tunisia, the battleground for the final struggle on North African soil between the Allied and Axis forces was now in the hands of American and British armies.

Every war suffers the agony and ecstasy of rumors and this outpost in the dry, arid country of North Africa was no different.

The army was getting ready to invade Europe and the rumors were flying fast and furious.

Where will they land? Sicily? Sardina? Naples? Rome? Each rumor set off a flurry of excitement that sent the soldiers in a spin.

"Will we join them?" Violet asked Hatty.

"We have to go wherever they land. They need us more than ever because wherever it will be there will be lots of blood shed."

Fear crossed Violet's face. "I guess we have to get a foothold on European soil if we want to end this war."

Hatty smiled at Violet, "In the meantime let's enjoy our fifteen minutes of peace. Who knows what fate has in store for us."

What Hatty didn't know and would never have imagined was that fate was already working full time across the Atlantic.

Chapter Twelve

The Pentagon- Washington D.C.

The Secretary of War smiled at the man seated around the table. He cleared his throat, "Gentlemen, the conflict in North Africa is over, our armies are now headquartered in Tunisia waiting for the next move. We must plan our strategy carefully. Our main objective is to gain a foothold on the European continent via Italy. The floor is open for discussion."

He sat down and looked around him at the assemblage of military power. The men, all Generals, were hand-picked by the President of the United States to help plan the moves and operations for all battle fronts.

They were all seasoned men. Battles were their sole purpose in life. They liked nothing better than to plan an invasion or blitz. They all smiled at the Secretary. This war was their life force.

General Davis, a one-star General, spoke first. "I'd like to show you," he got up and walked over to a huge wall map, "The best way to get a foothold on European soil."

He pointed to the northeast tip of Tunisia, a beach called Cap Bon. "This beach is less than ninety miles away from the Sicilian coast. From here we could send our amphibious forces and storm the coast of Sicily at Gela, Agrigento, Licata and Miranella."

The faces of the other men looked non-committal. "The beaches are small," He continued, "And the land behind them is mountainous. Therefore I suggest we have sufficient air power to cover the landing."

General Ross, a two-star General, got up from his chair and walked to the map. "I think you're making a big mistake by invading that treacherous island. The mountains are rugged and we will encounter a great deal of problems getting to Messina."

He looked around for approval but the faces remained passive.

These men were all powerful military men, all jockeying for political recognition after realizing they were passed over for Eisenhower, Patton, Bradley and Mac Arthur.

They were not on the actual battlefront but their paper front was powerful. They knew it and savored every moment of it. The Pentagon was a powerful place.

General Ross continued, "My suggestion is to invade Sardinia, the island west of the main land. From there we can invade Italy all along the west coast and gain a better foothold."

The faces remained passive.

The Secretary of War leaned forward on the table, his fingers laced together, rested his chin on his hands. He seemed to be saying, 'I'm waiting.'

From the far corner of the table, General Clifford, a one-star General now in his seventies stood up. "Gentlemen," His voice still strong and vibrant, "look at this map carefully."

He was now in front of the map with a pointer in his hand. "Sardinia is above Sicily. Once we get into Sicily, the main land is a ferryboat away."

All remained passive. These were all cagey men. They always wanted to be on the right side.

"Therefore I agree with General Davis. We invade Sicily. In the long run it will be easier and faster.

General Ross, his face a livid red, "Are you aware of the history of the island?"

The men all focused their attention on him.

"Of course," Answered General Clifford, "The people are suspicious and they don't care who the hell governs the island because they do as they damn well please."

The men shifted in their chairs uneasily. General Ross and General Clifford never liked each other and they were going to reject each other's plan no matter who was right.

The Secretary unlaced his fingers and leaned back in his chair.

General Ross continued angrily, "Those mountains are rugged and treacherous. From these mountains they see anyone and everyone trying to invade their shores."

General Clifford smiled. "True but if they want us to come in they can also pave the way and make it a cinch for us to set foot on European soil."

General Ross sputtered, "Those people think Mussolini is God."

"In the beginning, yes," Interrupted General Clifford, "But no more. The Sicilians are not happy that the Germans have taken over."

General Ross angrier than ever, "That island is sewed up tight by the mob and their word is law."

Clifford's face beamed, "Precisely. My plan is to get the mob to work with us."

The men all looked at him as if he was crazy. His smile became broader.

General Davis, who had taken a back seat after he initiated the original plan spoke up, "Clifford, are you suggesting we consort with mobsters?"

"Why not?" Replied Clifford, "We'll just consider them mercenaries. Every war ever fought had it's lot of mercenaries."

The Secretary of war leaned forward and laughed, "How do we get these so-called mercenaries?"

Clifford smiled a smile of conspiracy "Leave it to me."

State Penitentiary, New York State, April 1943

The prison loomed out of the landscape like a mean gray giant. The winds, still frosty from a long, cold winter, lashed and scratched at everything in its path. Its meanness refused to abate despite the warming April sun.

The bus ground to a halt in front of the entrance gate and the doors blew open almost in defiance. The passengers filed out silently, their faces reflecting the ravages of hardship and sorrow.

They were the families and friends of the toughest incarcerated people in New York State-murderers, rapists, bank robbers, crooks, pimps-the most hardened men in the sub-culture of America's shady world.

In spite of this, the innocent victims came to see them.

A small elderly man in a neat black overcoat, his left empty sleeve tucked neatly into the pocket, stiffly descended the steps and walked uncertainly up the pathway.

He hesitated, would have lingered, but the people behind him gently nudged him to move on.

When he arrived at the entrance. The guards, indifferent to the anguished faces, gruffly demanded identification.

"Your name, prisoner's name and relationship," The hard faced guard growled.

He gave them his name and told them the prisoner's name. "He is my Godson," The man replied tremulously.

The guard looked him over and seeing his empty sleeve signaled to another guard.

The line ground to a halt.

"Take your coat off," The guard ordered. Two more guards moved in and trained their rifles at him as he slowly unbuttoned his coat.

All eyes were riveted on him. He slid the coat off his body and held it by the collar. The guard took the coat. "Now take off your jacket," The hard faced guard demanded officiously.

The jacket, a two button style, came off quickly. He stood there with the jacket in his hand. His neat white shirt with one sleeve was tucked into the belt of his pants.

The guard quickly frisked him, inspected his coat and jacket and handed them to a guard. "You can pick these up on your way out."

The old man nodded and proceeded down the corridor to the visitor's waiting room.

The guard watched the man with great interest, then turned to the other guards and whispered cautiously, "You can tell when the big guy is losing his place. They send the old relative to visit."

The old man sat down on the long bench with other visitors and waited for his name to be called.

"They gave you a rough time out there, " A hoarse voice next to him whispered.

The old man turned. The hoarse voice belonged to a hard-looking woman with a wrinkled face. The face was heavily made up to hide the ugliness, which instead aggravated the look.

'Whiskey and cigarettes,' The old man mused. This one is no stranger to dark corners. Be careful what you say,' He reminded himself.

With dignity and his voice just above a whisper, shrugged, "There are some things in life you have to accept."

"How did it happen?" The harsh voice brazenly asked pointing to his sleeve.

"I fell under a trolley car when I was a kid," He answered unfeelingly. She was about to continue the barrage of questions when he heard his name being called.

He rose stiffly and walked slowly towards the door to the inner visiting room. He was just about to enter when the brazen voice shouted, "Lots of luck old man."

He entered a long narrow room with a wall running the whole length. The top half was thick mesh screening. These were called the 'visitor's screens.'

The old man sat down at a designated spot at the counter. A second later a door opened and his Godson was ushered in.

Although slender and of medium height his presence filled the room. Sharp features etched his face giving him a noble look. But it was the eyes, dark, magnetic and piercing that dominated and mesmerizing whoever came in contact with him.

He looked at the old man and his eyes narrowed.

The appearance of his Godfather meant bad news. They always sent this innocent –looking man with messages nobody wanted to deliver.

Like the time two-fingers Angie was skimming the top of the numbers take. The old man showed up and asked him what they should do.

"First find out where he stashed the dough then take him for a deep swim."

Ever since he was framed on a pimping charge and sent up to the big house, the younger men in the mob became cocky. But he was the boss and his advice was sought after and his orders carried out.

When two-fingers Angie's body was fished out of the East River, the authorities grilled him unmercifully.

"Hello," The old man smiled at the glowering prisoner.

The younger man didn't answer.

The old man smiled, "Aren't you going to greet your Godfather?"

The prisoner looked hard, "What the hell are you doing here?"

The old man smiled, "I heard rumors."

The prisoner frowned, "What kind of rumors?"

The old man lowered his voice a decibel and almost whispered, "The army is all over the street asking questions about you."

The dark eyes opened wide. "Army? What the hell for? What kind of questions?"

"Dumb questions," The man gestured with his hand, "Like where you were born. Do you have any relatives over on the other side. Things like that."

He looked at the old man as if he were crazy, "You know something , I think you're nuts."

"You gotta believe me, "The tremulous voice pleaded. "The word is all over the street that there's something big in the wind. Everybody's scared. What with Pearl Harbor and the war in North Africa. Nobody knows what they're after. But you gotta believe, nobody's talking."

He looked at the old man with disbelief.

The old man continued, "That's why I came. So you'd be prepared for whatever the feds got in mind."

The chiseled face didn't say a word. His mind deep in thought. 'The army? What the hell did they want with him?' Finally he looked at the old man and said, "O.K., go home, play cards and keep your ears open."

The old man smiled, got up stiffly and left.

The guards came and led the prisoner back to his cell.

The old man shuffled past the guards and handed him back his visitor's card. They gave him back his jacket and coat.

As he walked out the door, the hard-faced woman with the harsh voice was standing there.

She gave him a broad smile. He smiled back weakly. She watched him as he walked back slowly to the bus stop and climb aboard a waiting bus.

She then entered one of the public phone booths outside the gate and closed the glass door. She dropped some coins in the slots and gave the operator the number. A few seconds later, the harsh voice whispered into the receiver, "He's been tipped off."

Governors Office, New York City

The two officers striding smartly into the New York City office of the Governor attracted little attention. It was a nation at war. The sight of military was common place.

All kinds of people came here. Some seeking changes in legislation. Others, favors for political endorsements and vote deliverance. It was a busy office and the Governor spent a great deal of time here when legislation was not in session at Albany.

The secretary announced the officers and ushered them into the walnut-paneled office. The star on one of the men's shoulder indicated the importance of these men.

"Sit down, Gentlemen," The Governor smiled, "What can I do for you?"

General Castleton spoke immediately and without any introduction. The U.S. Pentagon wants you to release a certain person now incarcerated in one of your prisons in upstate New York."

The Governor looked puzzled. "Who? Why?" He asked with a hint of uneasiness in his voice.

The General replied briskly, "I can only tell you who. I can't tell you why."

"Gentlemen," The Governor tried to sound very officious, "It's not that easy. Some prisoners can never be released. Others must have a very good reason to go before a parole board."

"We understand, Governor," The General replied, "But it's a matter of military intelligence."

The Governor became irritated. Ever since Pearl Harbor the military was showing a lot of political muscle. "Who's the prisoner? The Governor asked icily, his lips tightening into a thin line.

The General showing no emotion, stated firmly the prisoner's name.

The Governor was stunned. "Gentlemen you must be joking. This man is the biggest hoodlum in this country."

It was the victory and crowning glory of his district attorney days when it had taken every bit of strategy and low manipulation to get this man, head of a crime organization, behind bars. Now the army brazenly walks in and demands his release.

The Governor got up from his chair, placed his hands on the desk, leaned forward towards the men and with anger choking him, stated with emphasis on each word, "If I release this man every newspaper in the world will be headlining the news."

He straightened up and began pacing behind his desk. The furrows in his brow deepening with every step. "The repercussions will be enormous." His pace quickened. He turned to the General and whispered, "I'll be impeached."

"That's the spoils of the war," The General replied without emotion, "The papers will arrive tomorrow by messenger. Sign them. You have no choice. When a nation is at war certain concessions must be made. This is one of them."

The two men got up from their chairs, "Good day, Governor," The General smiled, Don't let this upset you. I'm sure you'll be able to handle this quietly and without any publicity." The men marched out without a backward glance.

The Governor was fuming. How would this affect his bid for the presidency? How could he keep this quiet? He sat down in his chair, rage boiling within him. How dare they ask him to do this unspeakable act. Why was the army so interested in this man? What could he possibly do for them?

Well he wasn't going to take this sitting down. He picked up the phone.

A week later the prisoner was in his cell reading. He still couldn't get the old man's message out of his mind. One thing was certain. He was still a very important man. Important enough for the army to be interested.

'Why the hell would the army turn to the streets. Any information they wanted could easily be obtained from the district attorney's office. Something big was in the wind. He could feel it in his bones.

He tried to concentrate on the book's plot when a guard appeared at his cell door. "Come on," The guard commanded, "The warden wants to see you."

He entered the warden's nicely appointed (a design trade phrase) office. He never failed to notice the newest furnishings that were constantly added or replacements for the warden's enjoyment. Even the art on the walls changed with regularity.

Sitting in front of the carved mahogany desk were two military men. Each had a star on his shoulder.

He knew instantly that the old man's message had a measure of truth to it.

The warden smiled and told him to take a seat. This really was good news, or was it? He never saw a smile on the warden's face.

"These gentlemen," Began the warden, "Are from the U.S. Army." He pointed to a bald-headed man, "General Harold Castleton ," And then to a white-haired man with cloudy blue eyes, "And this is General Edward Banks."

They all nodded in acknowledgment.

The warden cleared his throat and spoke slowly, "These gentlemen would like to talk to you privately." He turned to the military men, "I'll leave you with the prisoner," emphasizing the word prisoner. "I'll be in my outer office." The warden closed the door behind him quietly.

The military men looked the prisoner over carefully a non-committal look on their faces.

Suddenly General Castleton spoke, slowly and concisely nearly knocking the prisoner off his feet.

"How would you like to be a free man?"

A week later sitting in a military transport smiling broadly was Sonny Adamo (aka) Adams winging his way to Africa.

Chapter Thirteen

Tunisia

The babble of voices filled the air with accents from New York City streets, mid-western plains and quiet southern towns. Above the din, quick and sharp Arabic phrases cut through the sounds with a fiery swiftness.

Life among the natives slowly drifted back to peacetime existence bringing with it the colorful, exotic beat of a languid, intoxicating world.

Mesmerized American soldiers, enjoying some rest and relaxation, added a new dimension of excitement to the land of Arabian nights.

Fantasy wove its mystic, silken thread into the crude, sharp edges of reality and lured its victims into its lair.

Vinny James, a.k.a. Vincent Giacome, stood outside General Headquarters waiting to be called inside. He couldn't figure out why he was called to appear before the Colonel.

He was only a corporal in the division of the United States 8th Army Regiment. He took care of supplies, following the infantry as they fought their way across the African desert.

There was lots of stealing, bartering and bribing and he did his share without being obvious. It was a way of life in this arid, dusty hell hole.

Perhaps they found out and were going to punish him for it. Hell, one didn't go to the guard house for a pack of butts. Nevertheless, Vinny was nervous. So nervous he didn't notice the female medic who couldn't take her eyes off him.

Finally a Sergeant called and ushered him into the building.

The medic watched him disappear inside. Her heart racing wildly, she went to the Sergeant ,"Would you tell me where that soldier went?" Pointing to the vanishing soldier.

"I could," The soldier replies, "But you have to say please and tell me what your name is."

"Please and my name is Violet Gilbert." The soldier smiled broadly, "Hello Violet. His name is Vinny James and my name is…"

She turned and walked into the building, her heart beating wildly. 'My God but he is gorgeous . I've have to meet him' She mused.'

Vinny was ushered into the Colonel's office, "Corporal Vincent Giacomo, Sir."

Vinny's handsome face tried without success, to hide the nervousness and puzzlement he felt.

"Sit down, Corporal," The Colonel ordered in a voice that sounded gently amused, despite its gruffness.

Vinny sat down in a high backed chair facing a long, ornately carved desk. The Colonel, a square faced , heavy jawed man sat behind the desk in a matching , carved chair. A manila folder lay on the desk with Corporal Vincent Giacomo a.k.a. Vinny James written across it.

Vinny felt he was facing Satan's henchmen on judgment day.

What the hell was he, Vincent Giacomo, a.k.a. Vinny James, doing here sitting in front of an American Colonel. His mind raced into every corner of his brain looking for a reason.

The Colonel picked up some papers from the folder, scanned the contents, his face showing no expression.

Vinny's mind rolled back over the years. He grew up on tenth Avenue in the Hell's Kitchen section of New York City. His home was a railroad flat on the top floor of a red brick tenement building that was scrunched between other tenements. It seemed at times that the old buildings leaned on each other for the protection against the dirt, poverty and violence.

The Hell's Kitchen section of the city was a depository where the poorest of humanity was forced to live. Some got out. Most didn't. Vinny always knew he was going to get out but he didn't count on a war to do it.

Young, tough and sinuous, he was respected by neighborhood gangs all along tenth Avenue from forty second street up to fifty second.

He was also very handsome. His rugged features were highly accented by chameleon color eyes that picked up and reflected the colors and moods that surrounded him.

The girls went wild when he went down the street. He had the ingredients that would send him in any direction he wanted to go.

One of those directions came one day when Fats O'Toole, a bookie, invited him to the diner for a cup of coffee.

"I like your style kid, " O'Toole said after he finished dumping five teaspoons of sugar into his coffee.

"Thanks," Vinny replied, a little awed. This man was a big shot in the eyes of the young man.

"How old are you?" O'Toole asked while he stirred the mound of sugar in his coffee.

"Eighteen," Vinny answered with hesitation.

"Finished school?" Fats kept stirring the mound of sugar in his coffee, his eyes intent on the liquid in the cup.

Vinny was fascinated. 'What a hell of a production. It was only a cup of coffee.'

"Just graduated from St. Michaels."

"Pretty good," O'Toole pursed his lips, satisfaction mixed with curiosity. "Unusual for a tenth Avenue kid, isn't it?" His hands still pushing the spoon around in his cup.

Vinny flushed. "My mother has this crazy idea in her head that the Giacomo family is going to produce a priest.," His voice choking on the last word.

"Well your education shows. You have a great speaking voice," Fats declared looking up for the first time.

Vinny began to feel uncomfortable. Did Fats hear about Vinny's imitation of him? It was a well known fact along the street that Vinny could imitate anybody and everybody. All he had to do was listen once and he could pick up the accents, the inflections and even the tone of the voice of the person. You could swear he was Irish when he mimicked Fats. He even imitated his swishing, waddling walk. He was so good at it, some people suggested he go to Hollywood and be in pictures.

Fats looked intently at the young man. Behind all that fat and swish, he was a smart man. "Well?" He asked, "Are you going to become a priest?"

"Hell no," Vinny answered sharply. Perhaps too sharply. Fats smiled knowingly.

"What does your mother say?"

"She doesn't know yet." Vinny's eyes turned a steely gray then a light green. "Getting a kid into a seminary is tough. The Diocese thinks we're all bums."

A smile played around his mouth. "You have to know the right people. My mother doesn't know anybody," Vinny concluded with satisfaction.

"What do you want to do?" Fats eyes squinted into slits making his fat face look like a badly decorated pumpkin.

Vinny shrugged his shoulders. "Right now I just want to make some money. A guy needs money to dress up and take the dames out."

"How right you are," Fats agreed, "And you can make some money working for me."

"Work for you?" Vinny was flattered and scared. 'Did Fats think enough of this kid to work for him?'

"There's nothing much you have to do," Fats said, "I need someone to drive me around. Someone who knows how to park a car. One who looks good behind a wheel."

Vinny glowed.

Fats continued, "I just bought myself a Packard Touring car. They don't make them anymore. But I love antique cars. They stand out. That's what I like, 'to stand out."

Vinny's heart pound rapidly. Money and a ritzy car, what luck!

"Think you can do it kid?" Fats looked intently at him over the rim of the cup he was putting to his lips.

"You bet I can," Vinny answered gleefully.

The next day he started driving Fats around. That's the day he changed his name from Vincent Giacomo to Vinny James.

He told his mother he was a chauffeur for a big manufacturer, driving him to all his factories. His mother believed him. This was the son who was going to be a priest. His father was too tired to question him closely.

Each day the older Giacomo went down into the dank, dark subway system and cleaned miles and miles of track. He coughed a lot and his tired body couldn't handle the stress of raising his children with a firm hand. He left that to his wife, a strong, determined woman. Whatever she said was fine with him.

Most of the time he longed for the clean, beautiful air of his Sicilian homeland. There he was able to carry on his beloved profession of puppetry. He loved going from town to town delighting and enchanting people.

The lure of America was so great, he emigrated with thousands of other Sicilians to follow the golden dream. But the dream soon faded to a dull ache when the puppeteer realized that Americans weren't interested in his craft.

Like the rest of the immigrants, he folded up his dream and put it away.

Vinny vowed he wasn't going to follow in his father's footsteps. He flourished in his job with Fats. He bought clothes, which set off his rugged, handsome body and he had all the girls he wanted. He also helped out with money at home.

He was just staring to get a good grip on himself when Pearl Harbor was bombed.

Vinny was one of the first to be drafted. Everybody was going and that took the bite out of it for him. It was a good chance to see something else instead of the narrow confines of his neighborhood.

From his first day at Fort Dix, Vinny was the star of the outfit. Starting with his imitations of the doctors at the induction center, down to the Sergeant in charge, Vinny kept the soldiers laughing. He became the leader of the group.

When he showed up on tenth Avenue in his army khakis, the girls rallied around him in great numbers. Fats promised him his job back when the war was over.

He learned a lot of things in the army. One of the most difficult was to learn to take orders from Sergeants with southern drawls he could barely understand.

He had to learn to deal with fellows who grew up in small towns and farms. To him they were slow movers and thinkers. To them, he was a tough city guy with a touch of class. He advised them in girl actions. He even showed them how to look good in army fatigues.

They told him about fishing, hunting and other activities that always seemed so remote. Somehow they sounded like his mother and father when they talked about their hilltop village in Sicily.

The Colonel cleared his throat and Vinny's mind jolted to a halt. "Corporal," The big faced man asked, "Do you speak the Sicilian dialect?"

The question hit Vinny with an exploding impact. It was a question Americans never asked. He was asked many times if he spoke Italian, but never, if he spoke the Sicilian dialect. Very few Americans even knew there was such a language.

He gave the man facing him a searching look.

The man's face remained impassive.

Vinny swallowed hard, "Yes," He answered, his voice showing nervousness.

"Good," The replied, "We need you for a very important mission."

Vinny's head jerked up straight.

The Colonel smiled, "You'll be accompanying a very able person. Together you will accomplish a very important task for the U.S. We'll let you know all the details as soon as your partner gets here."

What Vinny didn't know was that at that very moment his partner was winging his way across the Atlantic.

Chapter Fourteen

Vinny needed a drink. This was too much for him to absorb. He wandered down to a G.I's favorite watering hole hilariously nicknamed, 'The Camel's Hump.'

Vinny sipped his beer slowly as he surveyed the faces at the crowded bar. Housed alone in a walled area the stuccoed cubed building sat low on the ground barely discernible on the main road leading into the city.

Tunisian girls, many with European backgrounds flocked there to make money with their only possession, their bodies. Everybody was Joe to them.

"Hey Joe," They would shout, "Wanna fuck?" The first time Vinny was propositioned, he froze.

He loved girls. He loved going to bed with them. He loved wrapping his hard, muscular body around a soft, rounded female.

From his first sexual encounter at fourteen to his present active sex life, Vinny regarded women as a gift. All his toughness disappeared when he had a girl in his arms. He was in another dimension. A dimension of light and spiritual loftiness, where he floated with joy that lasted hours after the girl was gone.

A hard looking girl sidled over to him, "Hey Joe."

He cut her short. "Forget it I'm busy tonight."

He turned his attention to his drink when he felt a pair of eyes looking at him. He looked into the direction of the gaze.

His heart flipped. 'Ah, yes,' he sighed. Beautiful, young and definitely American with soft features on a finely boned face. His eyes were so riveted to the almond shaped, smoky blue eyes he barely noticed she was wearing army fatigues. A few moments later he noticed the Shepherds Followers medic patch on her sleeve.

He raised his glass to her. She smiled. In two seconds he was by her side. "Hi, I'm Vinny James."

She smiled, "Hi, I'm Violet Gilbert." He waved his glass, "What is a pretty girl like you doing in a hell hole like this?"

She laughed, "We're at war, remember?"

"Who can forget?" Vinny couldn't take his eyes off her. She was definitely American but there was a strong hint of the orient in her smoky blue eyes.

He felt as if he was handed a gift. A gift on a silver platter. This one he had to have., but the Shepherds Followers puritans? 'Go slowly,' He cautioned himself, this girl has made his heart flip and she is everything he ever dreamed of-smashing good looks with a softness that promised magical nights. He didn't want to lose her.

"I see by your patch you belong to the Followers.

She nodded.

"Is it true what they say about your outfit?"

She laughed, "Tell me, what do they say about us?"

A slow smile spread over his handsome features. His eyes turned a soft gray, "They say that you are a loving, gentle people and you love your neighbors."

She laughed softly, "Yes, it's true, but there are some of us, when confronted with adversity, are not so gentle."

"Then you've got spirit. I like that."

He raised his glass, "To a gentle, loving girl, who when confronted with adversity, is a hell raiser." She raised her glass and they both laughed.

They were sipping their beers when he placed his hands on her elbow and nudged her into the direction of the door. "There's a garden stuck onto this place. Why don't we take our drinks out there." She nodded in agreement.

The tropical night air was balmy. A silence fell over the vast outdoors. "Isn't it strange," She whispered, "The night is so quiet, you would never think there's a war going on."

"They stopped it just for us." He answered quietly.

She smiled , "Tell me a little about yourself."

"Only if you promise to tell me all bout yourself," He smiled.

"It's a deal," She put out her hand, he took it and squeezed it gently.

He told her about his neighborhood. His mother's desire for him to become a priest. His friends, everything except that he was a chauffeur for a mob figure.

He told her the same story he told his mother, that he drove for a president of a big manufacturing plant around to his various enterprises.

"Now that I bared my soul to you, it's your turn."

She shrugged her shoulders, "There's little to tell. Growing up in a religious home is routine. You pray a lot. You learn to be an obedient servant of God, even it kills you." Then she began to giggle.

"Praying and being obedient is funny?" He looked at her puzzled.

"No," She laughed, "Aunt Hatty and I played this great game. Whenever we were alone we sang and danced all the popular songs. We went to the picture show and carnivals an did all kinds of fun things except pray and be obedient."

"In other words, you let your hair down," He laughed.

"That we did. Aunt Hatty insisted."

"Your Aunt Hatty sounds terrific."

"She is. She's stuck in a loveless marriage and makes up for it in many other ways."

"Good for her, she's beginning to sound even more terrific.

"She is and she's been a good mother to me. Loving and full of fun. Uncle Josh too."

Vinny began to sing, "Da da dum dum. The plot thickens, Tell me more."

Violet started from the beginning with her arrival at the Gilbert household. Her trips to New York in the summers, her Uncle Joshua, the brilliant tax lawyer who at this moment was in Switzerland working for the government and his love and relationship with Mimi.

Vinny laughed out loud, "And you said there was nothing to tell." He hugged and said, "You are a wonderful bundle of life and mystery but tell me how did you get to be a medic?"

"I'm a sign language teacher, I teach deaf children. I wanted to serve my country and the only way I could do it was to become part of a medical team."

"What kind of religion is it that sends pretty, young girls into the heat of battle." He was puzzled. The girls in his huge extended family were kept at home. They would never send their females into any kind of danger zones. That's why none of the girls in his family were allowed out at night alone.

"We're a passive people," Violet answered, "But we're always in the middle of a battle. That's where we belong."

"And where is this Uncle, your father's brother and your Aunt's unloving husband at right now?"

"Where else?" She laughed sarcastically," At home safe and sound running the units from his office and enjoying all the comforts of home and lovers."

Vinny edged closer to her. She didn't offer any resistance. Violet was determined to savor life to the fullest before she settled into the Followers strict regime.

She thought many times that she would leave and go to New York but she didn't want to leave Hatty. So she decided to stay and enjoy the life that her aunt was steering her into.

The stars glowed and twinkled in the inky blackness. Nearby a jasmine bush in full tropical bloom sent forth its fragrance enveloping them with its intoxicating scent.

Vinny took Violet in his arms and buried his head into her neck. His lips played gently against her skin slowly as if in time with their own heart beat. She put her arms around his neck and pressed her body against his.

He tightened his grip and whispered, "Let's share this night of magic."

She loosened her grip, tilted her face towards his and answered dreamily, "Oh yes."

Chapter Fifteen

Sonny Adams and Vinny James shook hands. The Colonel sat down behind his desk, smiled and wondered. A big time hood and a God damn handsome street kid. It was like adding more dynamite to an already potent explosive.

Since his release from prison, Sonny had been thoroughly briefed...what, why, who, where and when this assignment had to be carried out.. Every move was gone over and over so that everything would go according to plan.

Sonny looked Vinny over, "Hey kid," How come you talk so fancy. Not like a kid from tenth Avenue."

Vinny went into a mimic of Jimmy Cagney, Edward G. Robinson and Orsen Wells whose well rounded words and dulcet tone Vinny captured beautifully.

"Ah, an actor," Sonny laughed, "you wanna be in pictures?"

Vinny turned serious, "When this lousy war is over, why not? I hear the dough is good."

Sonny turned to the Colonel, "The kid looks good to me. We'll do O.K."

The Colonel handed Sonny a large envelope, "Everything you need to know is there. There are a lot of risks, but this is war, risks have to be taken."

Sonny smirked at the Colonel, "My whole life's been one big risk."

"You have about two weeks to prepare," The Colonel ignored Sonny's remark. "We'll keep you informed."

"Come on kid," Sonny turned to Vinny, "We've got a lot of work to do."

Outside the building Violet was standing by the Followers van. When she saw Vinny she waved.

"That's some good looking broad," Sonny chuckled, "I'd like to lay her right here on the ground. Now!"

"Let's get something straight," Vinny hissed, bravado overtaking his awe and fear of the biggest crime boss in America, "We have to share a lot of things during this mission but she's not one of them."

"You got some kind of feeling for this one, kid?"

"Yes," Vinny answered softly.

"O.K.," Sonny replied, "She's all yours. There's plenty of dames around. I hear they know how to use their muscles. You know lotta contractions," Sonny howled.

Violet walked over to them and Vinny introduced Sonny as Nick Roman.

"Hi, Nick," Violet held out her hand.

"Hi, Violet," Sonny replied, his heart skipping a beat. Can it be? Those eyes were a dead give away. It was many years and she was just a little girl. 'Take it easy,' He told himself. Life is full of strange twists.'

He smiled, "Pleased to meet you. Why don't we all have a drink at one of those flea bag bars."

Before Vinny could reply, Violet said, "Not a bad idea, this place sure dries up your throat."

Vinny took her by the arm, a scowl crossing his face as the three of them walked down the sand-covered street.

Sonny had taken the first sip of beer when a man in army fatigues with an Associated Press patch on his sleeve came over to their table. Looking at Sonny he said, "He soldier has anyone ever told you that you are the spitting image of Sonny Adams."

Sonny looked up and smiled, "Who the hell is Sonny Adams?"

"The biggest gangster in America." The correspondent boasted.

"Would I be here if I was him?" Sonny asked indignantly.

"No, I guess not," The correspondent replied and left.

"Do you really look like this Sonny Adams?" Violet asked thinking and puzzling why he looked so familiar.

"Naw," He answered. Then he smiled mischievously, "Well, maybe a little bit. We both have sneaky looking eyes." And he laughed heartily. Hi raised his glass and they joined him in a silent toast.

A buxom girl sidled over to the table and stood over Sonny, "Hey poppa, you wanna fuck?"

"Sure, why not," He smirked, "Wanna do it right here on the floor?"

The girl smiled slyly, "No, upstairs. Nice bed. Fan, too."

"Well wadda you know. You get a breeze with a squeeze."

He handed Vinny the envelope and his wallet after extracting a ten dollar bill. "These girls are expert rollers. Hold my stuff, I won't be long."

Vinny took Violet's hand in his, "I'm sorry about this but I'm stuck with him for a while. We have to go on a mission. I don't know if we can have much time together, we have a lot of work to do."

Violet squeezed his hand back, "We'll make the time," She assured him.

A group of rowdy soldiers entered the bar and the noise level rose to high pitch, making conversation impossible.

The young couple contented themselves by just being together.

The Shepherds Followers unit was assigned a small building on one of the narrow streets in the heart of Tunisia. They used the building as a supply post and living quarters.

The small cubed building was sheltered from the street with a high wall. A high wooden gate led into a small courtyard where the vans and ambulances were able to park.

Here they were safe from the street thieves who stole and stripped everything in sight.

Violet pulled up to the gate in a small jeep and honked the horn. The gate swung open and Violet roared into the yard.

Hatty was by the window watering one of a dozen aloe plants. "That girl," She chuckled, "Has enough energy to win the war if they let her."

Something stirred within her whenever she looked at Violet. Was it her youth? Her beauty or her spirit? Or maybe it was the way Violet had changed her life.

She looked at Violet coming up the path, a glow about her that could mean only one thing. That girl was going to bed with someone. Hatty waited for this day when this sweet girl would find love, even for a short while, like her affair with Sonny Adams.

'Ah, Sonny,' She mused, 'Where did you disappear to? No matter where I was or who I was with, you were always with me.

Everyone paled beside you. That was a love she carried deep in her heart. A love she knew she could never share with the world.

"Lucky girl," she cooed to the plants, "Maybe that's what you need, you drooping little plants…a mate…I'll see what I can do for you. Maybe that's what I need too," She laughed adding more water to the plants. "I'll see what I can do for both of us."

Violet walked in dropped papers on the desk, "Hi, Hatty, requisitions for some supplies."

Hatty put down the watering can and walked over to the desk.

"I hope your list is conservative. Things may have slowed down a bit, but I'm sure they'll pick up. Wars have a habit of doing just that."

She picked up the papers and scanned the list. "Seems normal to me," And in the next breath, "Who's your friend?

Violet looked up quickly, "What friend?"

"Whoever you're fooling around with," Hatty answered still looking at the list.

Violet's face turned a bright red, "What makes you say that?"

"Honey," Hatty put down the list and looked Violet straight in the eyes. "I've been there. Whenever you spend your life in the world's most forgotten corner, helping people who haven't the vaguest idea what you're all about and who couldn't care less, you fool around whenever you can."

Violet sat down and gave Hatty a long look. A smile crossed her lovely features. "I'm not fooling around, Auntie, he is so beautiful. I'm madly in love with him."

"I can see that, you're glowing like a Christmas tree. Don't ever turn your back on love, sweetie, you and I have to grab our happiness no matter where. Just remember one thing, we can't live happily ever after."

"Oh, I know that Auntie, you've told me that many times and I'm following your advice." Her smile grew broader, "He has a friend. An older man," The words rushed out enthusiastically.

"He's not a General, is he?" Hatty screwed up her face, "They're so regimented, even in bed, and," And she pointed a finger at Violet, "They map everything out first."

Aunt and niece looked at each other and laughed loudly.

Hatty leaned back in her chair and tried to appear nonchalant, 'Damn it,' she thought, 'It's been a long time. Wonder what he's like. Sure could use some fun. I've been working too hard.'

Violet interrupted her thoughts, "You'll like him Hatty, he's distinguished looking with gray hair and a little rough around the edges and there's a certain exciting element and familiarity about him I can't explain."

"Bring him around," Hatty smiled, "I'm beginning to droop like those plants."

"By the way," Hatty opened up a drawer, "I received some news you may not like."

Violet stopped short and turned around.

"They're calling you back home," Hatty scowled, "It seems that idiot they're trying to team you up with doesn't like the idea of you being in the middle of exploding bombs and diving fighter planes, not like my darling husband who wished one would fall right on my head."

Violet's face turned pale.

"They think," Hatty continued, "You'll be just as effective, not happy but effective, in the Arizona desert on some Indian Reservation."

An angry look crossed Violet's face and her smoky blue eyes threw off silver sparks.

"I'm not leaving all of this to go to a dull place where the children are not interested in our damn religion, which by the way, we sanctimoniously try to shove down their throats."

"Calm down, Violet," Hatty put her arms around the angry girl," Anger won't help you. If you want to stay, and you've got a good reason now, do what the Generals do."

"Such as?"

"Map out a plan," Hatty answered, "Plan it coolly and calmly."

A slow smile spread over Violet's face, "Thanks Auntie, I'll try to do that."

She was going out the door when Hatty called after her, "Don't forget your friend's friend."

Back in the jeep anger took over Violet, 'Damn I'm a big girl now, nobody's going to run my life for their own purposes.'

She put her foot on the clutch, turned the ignition key, shifted into first and gunned the motor. She made a sharp U-turn in the small courtyard. The man at the gate opened it quickly and shook his head as the jeep roared past him.

Hatty recognized Sonny the moment she saw him. Her heart pounded wildly and her breath was almost literally taken away. She was just about to say, "Hello Sonny," when Vinny introduced his as Nick Roman.

She knew immediately something big was in the wind.

Because he was introduced as Nick Roman, she went along with the masquerade.

Sonny's heart pounded wildly. The one girl in the world he never forgot, a girl he kept tucked in the corner of his heart, was miraculously sitting across from him at a restaurant halfway across the world.

He looked at her and smiled. She was even more beautiful than when he last saw her in New York. To say she improved with age is an understatement. Those summers in New York were the salve that kept him sane during his incarceration.

Hatty smiled back. 'My God,' She thought, 'He looks a little pale but he's just as stunning and exciting looking as ever. Let him tell me what this is all about later in bed.'

The waitress placed the steaming dishes on the table and announced in fractured English, "Please to enjoy."

Hatty picked up her fork and mixed a small mound of cubed meat into her golden color cous cous. "I generally don't do this," She apologized, "It's bad manners but goat doesn't taste like lamb."

Sonny chuckled, "It doesn't look like goat to me. It looks more like that animal I ran over today."

Vinny glanced at Violet. She smiled back. 'How nice,' He thought, 'She's not squeamish.'

Hatty took a mouthful, "It's goat."

"Good," Sunny nodded, "Then I'll eat it."

From the moment Sonny and Hatty met hey kept up their charade. Both were anxious to be alone with each other. There was a lot of catching up to do.

Hatty sighed, "It's always during a lull in my work that I wish I was back in New York eating and drinking the wonderful variety of cuisine available there."

Vinny and Sonny simultaneously asked, "Are you from New York?"

"No of course not," Hatty laughed, "Our religious cult, if you want to call it that wouldn't have a ghost of a chance in the cosmopolitan melting pot. We just have our school for the deaf there because it's something we're very good at."

Sonny smiled knowingly, "I'll bet you are."

Hatty continued, "Our families became members because it was necessary way back then. Kansas had two families to every twenty miles.

"Why the hell do you stay there? Sonny asked incredulously. "I get the feeling you'd rather be somewhere else like right in the heart of Broadway."

Hatty laughed cynically, "Believe it or not, we're not all that religious, in the sense you know religion. We quote the bible a great deal but only for our own benefit."

Sonny pointed his fork at Hatty, "One thing I can say about you Hatty, you're honest."

Violet who up to this point had not said a word joined in defensively, "But our work takes us all over the world where we're needed, just as we're needed here."

They all gave her their attention. She continued, "We won't bear arms, but we're always in the middle of a battle whether it's war or a natural disaster." She paused, looked at Sonny and Vinny defensively and stated, "That's our religion."

"Well," Sonny winked at Vinny, "Then if you're all that holy roly, then we're holy roly too."

Hatty raised her glass, Also it's convenient and we pay no taxes."

Sonny leaned over to her and said, "You're a girl after my own heart. I don't like paying taxes either" He clinked his glass to her, "I'd like to hear more about your outfit. Why don't we take a walk after we finish eating. I'm sure they wanna," pointing to Violet and Vinny, "Be alone."

Hatty smiled broadly, "I'll be delighted to acquaint you with my life style."

They left the restaurant and strolled slowly to a small square. Buildings whose windows had been darkened now showed gleaming lights.

Mellow with food and wine, they walked silently, each in their own thoughts. They had reached a corner of the square when Hatty turned to Sonny, "Oh Sonny, where have you been all this time?"

"In hell," He took her in his arms and held her tightly. "I never stopped loving you, I guess you know who I really am."

"I always knew," Hatty smiled, "But I didn't care. In my eyes you weren't what the papers said you were. You are and always will be the man in my heart. I Love you Sonny. When I thought I lost you forever, my heart shut down."

He drew her closer to him. "Tell me everything you did since the last time I saw you."

"It's a long, long story," Hatty sighed, "It'll probably take all night."

"In that case," Sonny whispered, "Why don't I buy a bottle of booze, rent a room and make ourselves comfortable."

"Are you going to be Sonny Adams or Nick Roman?" Hatty whispered back.

"Sonny Adams, I want to continue where we left off."

The room had a small bed, a night table with an oil lamp on it, a small round table and two chairs.

Sonny filled two cracked cups with scotch. He handed one to Hatty who was sitting coss-legged on the bed. She was barefoot and her straight skirt was rolled up to her torso.

She tasted the scotch, nodded in approval, filled her mouth and rolled the liquid slowly, moving her closed lips in and out.

"You can't ever imagine how much I love you Hatty," Sonny raised his cup to her.

"And you'll never know how much I missed you, dreamed about you, had sex with you in my dreams and how my heart hurt because I loved you so much."

He loosened his tie, "Man it's hot in here."

"We Americans are so dumb," Hatty quipped, "We're in the middle of the desert and we dress as if we're in the middle of Nebraska."

"You don't want to go in those long robes, do you?" Sonny laughed.

"Under those long robes," She giggled, "Are stark naked bodies."

"Then why don't we do what the natives do?" Sonny began unbuttoning his shirt. "But without the robes."

Hatty didn't move.

"Well?" He asked, "How about it?"

She smiled, "Undress slowly, Sonny, I want to watch you strip down to your bare skin."

He got up and began a slow imitation of a strip teaser.

Hatty watched him, this man who was a notorious gangster and her lover. A man who never left her heart. What a difference this was from her one night with Thorton. Thank God for men like Sonny who knew what women were all about and did something about it.

He loosened his belt, whipped it, stamped his feet and began doing a flamenco dance.

Hatty, who had been feeling the stirrings within her body the moment she laid eyes on Sonny, felt the weariness she had felt during the long months of war, leave her. She clapped her hands gleefully.

"Take it off," She chanted, "Take it off,' And began unbuttoning her blouse. He unzipped his fly and his pants fell to the floor.

"Why you wicked person," Hatty tittered, "You were stark naked under those pants all the time."

Sonny smiled broadly, "The natives aren't the only ones who are smart around here."

Hatty got off the bed and quickly and removed the rest of her clothes and slowly revolved around the room as if she were a model.

He took her in his arms and buried his lips into her neck. "It's been a hell of a long time since I had the pleasure of your company and my body is screaming for you."

"It's been a hell of a long time for me since I had the pleasure of your body," She whispered breathlessly.

She brought her hands from around his neck, interlaced her fingers and gently placed his swollen flesh in her cupped hands.

They walked slowly to the bed, his lips hungrily drawing in the flesh on her neck, shoulders, cleavage and nipples.

Her hands gently rolled the hard mass of flesh sending sensitive, strong yearnings surging through his body.

He felt the tension of his prison years float out of his body and a fiery warmth engulfed him making his body pulsate with burning desire.

They went to bed and in unison lowered their bodies to the hard mattress. She wrapped her legs around him as he slowly entered her, sinking his huge, hard flesh deep into her.

She sighed, pressed her opened mouth on his and slowly began sucking his tongue and contracting her pelvic muscles.

His senses reeled. She moved in rhythm with him as he buried his flesh deeper into her as the two became one in body and soul.

Sonny opened his eyes as the dawns light slowly filtered through the shutters. He raised himself on one elbow and viewed the results of the night before.

The almost full bottle of scotch was on the table, a telling sign, that this narcotic was not needed for their full night of passion.

Their clothes were strewn all over the floor. He looked down at the sleeping Hatty. Her face in repose was serene.

"What a beautiful woman she is," He murmured. Hatty's light brown hair, always severely combed back and tied into a knot, now lay loose and softly framed her face. With her softly rounded naked body, she reminded him of a renaissance painting.

He thought of the many woman he bedded. Most of them beautiful show girls from New York's famous night clubs. Actresses from Hollywood. All beautiful, all ready to please physically and all looking for the rainbow with the pot full of gold.

Going to bed with them only satisfied his ego.

He knew the difference, many years ago, when Hatty first went into his arms. She was spiritual. Her touch was gentle. Her response electric. Sonny shivered with delight. Every nerve in his body felt deliciously exquisite when he came in contact with her body. Scotch was a necessary requirement in all his other encounter. His sex life was always a matter of need. The bottle helped. Without it he couldn't perform. He realized he had no need for the strong liquor when he was with Hatty. The chemistry between them was explosive and electrifying.

He gently pushed back a strand of hair away form her face. "So help me God," He whispered, "You will always be part of my life."

Hatty opened her eyes, "And you were always part of mine," and opened her arms and embraced him, her warm body sending his nerves quivering.

They stayed in each other's arms savoring the exquisiteness of the moment.

She took his face in her hands, When I first found out who you really were I was devastated. But my love for you was so strong, I brushed it aside. I didn't know that side of your life and I didn't want to know. I only knew you for the wonderful, gentle lover you are and all the pleasure you brought to me with your body and generosity."

She kissed his face and pressed him closer to her, "We both lead very strange lives. There is so little joy in always being in the middle of sickness, holocaust and natural disasters. You are the only pleasure I ever had in my life. You're a gift from God."

"Really?" His face glowed.

"Really and I have no intention of caring what you do in your working life. I hope you don't care what I do in mine."

She loosened her hold letting her hands roam over his skin. He kissed her all over hungrily. Her hands wend their way down to his groin until she found, the hard, swollen mass. She began to massage them, rolling them gently, exquisitely. His flesh extended into a hard, long rod, ready to explode.

She put her body under him and guided the fiery appendage into her body. He sank deeply into her and her muscles contracted and clutched the hot flesh fiercely and rhythmically that sent both of them exploding with joy. The world with all its horror and problems disappeared. With a sigh they had reached their zenith.

For the next two weeks, Hatty, Sonny, Violet and Vinny lived in a world of fantasy. They soaked in the exotic Arab world where everything was color and sound. Strong, vibrant hues reflected the strong passions and impulses of its people, transferring it to the lovers.

Oranges, reds, yellows, even black radiated a sense of excitement running wild and untethered. Feelings ran deep as they expressed their emotions freely and passionately.

How ironic, Hatty thought, that she had to find love with a man more powerful than her father but from a different world. A world that shocked and fascinated at the same time.

And Violet, caught up in the same strange shocking dilemma was in a situation more complicated and frightening as the two females faced the world.

The night before Sonny and Vinny were departing for their mission, the two couples had dinner and then each went their separate way.

Sonny and Hatty to their trysting place, Violet and Vinny to their favorite inn outside of town where the European couple who ran the place prepared a quiet room overlooking a walled garden.

Here the young couple were able to spend the night away from the maddening crowds. The fragrance of blooming jasmine drifted through the room sending their senses reeling.

The young lovers held on to each other with a fiery passion not knowing whether this was the beginning or the end of their romance.

"I can't promise you anything at this time," Vinny holding Violet tightly, "But I know that wherever you are I will find you. I can't let you go."

"I can't see life without you," Violet sobbed, "They already have a husband waiting for me. Take me with you."

"I can't," Vinny hushed, "It's a military mission, Violet," He kissed her gently on the lips. "Don't let them run your life. Wait for me. I'll come and get you if it's the last thing I do."

The lovers spent the night wrapped in each other's arms dreading the coming of dawn when they had to part.

It was the same with Hatty and Sonny. Two star-crossed lovers who knew that their love had to be stolen from the clutches of destiny.

They made love all night long savoring each other's body with a lust and passion tinged with sadness.

Chapter Sixteen

The jeep carrying Sonny and Vinny arrived at Cap Bon just as the fishermen were ready to call it a day.

The driver pulled up in front of a small inn called Le Petite Auberge.

This is the end of the line," The Sergeant behind the wheel announced "My orders are to drop you off here."

The two men jumped out, took their duffel bags from the back seat and hoisted them over their shoulders. The jeep roared away in a cloud of dust.

"Well," Sonny grinned, "We'll never make history standing here like two jerks."

Vinny grinned back and in a clipped British accent replied, "Right-o-Sir."

Inside the inn, the big rough- looking Tunisian, of European lineage, and pock-marked face, registered them with insolent indifference. "All I have is a room in the Atlier," He droned, "Room 301," And handed them a key on a ring as big as a plate.

"Thanks a lot pal," Sonny snarled, "That's all I need today, is a hot box."

"The room catches the breezes from the sea." The Tunisian answered, his eyes still on the register book, "You won't be uncomfortable."

Sonny and Vinny climbed the big staircase up to the second floor, then up a smaller staircase which led to the attic room.

Sonny took a small gun out of a holster strapped just below his kneecap under his pant leg. He unlocked the door, turned the knob and kicked it wide open. He moved in cautiously, the gun cocked, ready to fire. A quick look and he motioned Vinny to follow him in.

"Do you always enter a room that way?"

"No, I let my bodyguards do that."

The room was a pleasant surprise. A huge poster bed loomed between two windows with a birds-eye view of the sea, an embroidered satin upholstered love seat graced the foot of the bed.

The other furniture included a highly polished round table, two upholstered chairs in the embroidered satin of the love seat, and an ornately carved desk. The floor was covered with a richly colored oriental rug.

"Well, wadda you know," Whistled Sonny, "A whore's bedroom," and threw his duffel bag on the satin bedspread. He sat on the bed and looked around.

Vinny walked around the room and touched each piece of furniture in awestruck wonder.

"You like it kid?"

"You bet," Vinny sighed, "This is the way I'd like to live the rest of my life."

"You could if you play your cards right."

"Everyone knows that," Vinny scoffed, "The luck comes in knowing when you have the right hand."

They both laughed.

Vinny was glad he was chosen to go on this mission with Sonny. If only the gang back home could see him now, Vinny James, in the company of the illustrious Sonny Adams.

"Wow," He swallowed hard. It suddenly hit him in what really big-time company he was with. He sat down on the plush covered bed and studied Sonny emptying his duffel bag.

Sonny, whose perception was razor-sharp, looked up and laughed. "I bet you never thought when you were driving Fats O'Toole around that you'd ever be in my company."

Vinny jumped off the bed like a rocket. "You knew that I wheeled Fats O'Toole around?"

"Sure," Sonny turned back to his duffel bag. "I did a lot of research and I picked you as my aide for this job. You came highly recommended."

"By who?"

"By whom," Sonny corrected. "Learn to speak the King's language correctly, you never know when you have to use it."

Vinny returned to the bed, sat down and shook his head in amazement, "Now I know why you're the top man."

"Thank you," Sonny pointed his hand with forefinger and thumb at Vinny. "O.K. kid, let's get started."

The two men sat down at the desk and began the arduous task of planning the intricate details that would make their mission a success.

Vinny picked each sheet up and read the contents carefully. "According to these plans we have plenty of help along the way."

"Maybe yes and maybe no," Sonny retorted. These military big shots sit around all day with their fingers up their ass."

Vinny looked up sharply.

Sonny continued, "I run a big operation back in the states, it reaches out to every port in the world. As a master planner, I can tell that some of these plans have weak spots."

"What are you going to do about it?" Vinny looked puzzled.

"Re plan it, kid, re plan it…my way."

Scanning the sheet without looking up, Sonny continued, "I knew their plans would have weak spots. That's why I insisted on a kid that grew up on the streets of New York. Only New York I said, or the deals not worth a shit."

Vinny put down the map he was reading. "I thought you were doing time?"

"I was," Sonny grinned. "We made a deal. I help out in this mission, they give me my freedom. They came to me because they knew they would be in a hell of a lot of trouble without my help."

Vinny looked puzzled. Sonny laughed out loud. "Does that surprise you, kid?"

"In a way," Vinny replied honestly.

I study a lot," Sonny continued, "I study everything I have to know that concerns my business. And because my business is all over the world, I have to do a lot of studying."

Vinny looked impressed.

Sonny looked up from the sheet he was reading, "Don't let my street talk fool you, it's one of my strong points. I learned how to speak correctly by listening to radio announcers. I can mingle with big businessmen and feel comfortable and talk with fish mongers down at the Fulton Street market always feeling comfortable."

Vinny shook his head in wonder.

Sonny pointed out the waters separating the African and European continents on the map. "This area is active with fishing boats from Africa and Sicily," Sonny's finger tracing the water's area. "The boats pull out in the dark of night spreading their nets behind them. When the night loses its darkness to the dawn, they return home with their catch."

Vinny was slightly confused, "What's that got to do with us?"

"Plenty," Sonny quipped, "The men that work these boats are tough, shrewd and ply these waters with a brilliant know how of every tide and currant at every hour of the day."

Vinny impressed with this knowledge, said, "How can that be? I understand they can't read or write."

"True, but they can add figures faster than any adding machine and analyze navigational waters and political situations with astuteness. They're born with a native intelligence of the water that surrounds their island."

Sonny looked up at Vinny and continued, "The German and Italian Commanders respect them and allow them the freedom to fish and use their knowledge for their sea missions."

"And we're going across the sea with these men?" Vinny asked incredulously.

Sonny laughed, "They move guns, liquor and hash freely. Their fees are high and they don't care who pays them. Also Sonny continued, "Cap Bon is the busiest fishing village on the North African coast."

"I could see that," Vinny quipped. I also see that the beaches are backed with soaring cliffs. I guess that means something, right?"

"Right and if you look closely," Sonny went on, "You'll notice its crannies and niches, a favorite resting place for migrating birds."

"And," Vinny interrupted.

Sonny laughed, "And a favorite place to hid a cache of contraband."

"What about the lighthouse?" Vinny asked, "Can't they spot what's going on from up there?"

"Sure," Sonny went to the window, "But the keepers of the house only look out on a clear day when they can see Sicily."

Vinny looked at Sonny with a dawning light in his eyes.

"Always research where you're going," Sonny pointed a finger at him, "What you have to do and everything, no matter how trivial it seems, otherwise, kid, you're up shit creek."

The two men fell silent when Sonny suddenly said, "By the way I like your girlfriend. She's got class."

Vinny grinned broadly, "Would you believe she belongs to that religious group?"

Sonny took a cigarette out of his shirt pocket and lit it. He took a few deep puffs and blew out a few smoke rings, all the while his eyes riveted on Vinny.

"Let me educate you a bit on people. Lot's of them are not what they seem. Take Violet. She's a Shepherds Follower. She's a medic. All these things may seem like an accident to you and that she was born in the wrong family. She wasn't."

Vinny's back went up." She's got a lot of spirit, most likely inherited,"Then a soft look shone from his eyes, "Do you think there's a chance we can get married after the war is over?"

"Never," Sonny answered briskly.

"What do you mean by never? Anger spreading over Vinny's face.

"Don't get mad at me kid. That's the way I see it. This war's a lark for her. She's enjoying every minute of it."

A look of disbelief rushed over Vinny's face.

"You have to understand," Sonny continued, "She's been bottled up all her life but her religion, what the hell they believe in, gives her the freedom to do whatever she wants, now that she's grown up."

Sonny put out the cigarette, crushing the butt inside a cut glass ashtray.

"She marries you and she becomes your wife, period. She marries a guy in her group and she flits around the whole world, all in the name of charity and God. Her husband? He won't utter a peep. You wanna know why? Because it works like a charm. She goes off in one place and he goes off in another and screws everything in sight."

Vinny's chiseled features quivered.

Sonny took another cigarette out of his pocket, lit a match and put it to the tip of the cigarette. He took a long drag, "You're lucky kid, enjoy her while you can. With her you've class with ass."

Vinny balled his fists ready to punch Sonny but Sonny was quick to respond. He grabbed Vinny's wrist and held him in a tight hold.

"I know your feelings are strong but I know what I'm talking about. I didn't get where I am by not observing people and their politics. Don't be too disappointed if things don't turn out the way you think they will."

Everything according to plan was ready. Sonny and Vinny spent the last few hours before departure trying to get some. Sleep.

Sonny slept soundly but Vinny tossing and turning found sleep impossible. He kept hearing Violet's voice begging him to come back to her. His heart ached at the memory of her burying her head into his shoulders and crying.

Sonny's advice about Violet's future disturbed him. The way he felt about her was different than any feelings he ever had with the other women in his life.

He also worried about the mission. He had a strange feeling about the whole thing. He knew they were going to make contact with the Sicilian overlords to pave the way for an American invasion but did they need him? What were they going to find when they reached Sciacca?

"It's a small fishing port," Sonny informed him, "With no beach. The houses come right up to the water."

"And how are we going to land in a port with no beach??"

Sonny snorted, "This place is no Coney Island or Brighton Beach: no boardwalks; no shlock stores. It's a serious fishing port. The boats pull right up to the buildings."

"Like Venice?"

"Sort of. The buildings are just as old but without the phony bologna mystique about it. Nobody but fishermen go there. It's the perfect place to land."

"And who are we going to contact, may I ask?"

"You may ask but you're not getting an answer. Just follow me and do as you're told."

"I still don't know why I'm going along on this mission. You've got everything down pat."

"True but you have a very important job to do and your part in it will determine the mission's success."

Vinny tossed and turned. 'What the hell was he supposed to do that was so important?

Zero hour finally arrived and the two men left the hotel and found a jeep waiting for them. It was past midnight. They rode a short distance and were let out on a deserted beach.

The two men looked at the driver suspiciously, "I was told to leave you here," The Sergeant apologized, "Those were my orders."

He jumped into the jeep and drove off in a cloud of dust.

"Well, I guess we wait," Sonny declared. Vinny reached into his pocket for a cigarette but Sonny stopped him cold. "Light that butt kid and we will be sitting ducks for anyone lurking out there and don't talk either," He hissed.

They sat in silence not daring to say a word when out of the watery darkness a small boat pulled up to the beach. A man got out, ran to them and motioned them to the boat.

They climbed in and a sturdily-built man at the oars greeted them in the Sicilian tradition, "Sa bene dia,"

Sonny returned the greeting with the reply, "Santo, Santo."

They rowed out into the inky darkness until a fishing boat loomed up out of the water. They clambered aboard and were quickly ushered into a dark corner piled with nets.

"If a patrol boat stops us," The man ordered, "Pile the nets around you."

"Will they search the boat?" Sonny inquired, a note of anxiety in his voice.

"Sometimes," The man answered nonchalantly, "But we take care of them and they leave quickly."

They moved through the darkened waters for three hours without an incident, when out of the darkness a patrol boat warning signal rang out as it pulled up alongside the fishing boat.

"Halt," A German voice ordered and two men climbed aboard. One man had the Nazi swastika on his arm band, the other was obviously a Sicilian fisherman.

"The German wants to know if you have anything other than fish on this boat," The Sicilian smirked.

"All we have is what we're catching," The burly man, who was evidently the owner of the vessel, replied.

"He wants to take a look," The fisherman gestured with his arm, "All around the boat."

Sonny and Vinny heard the conversation and knew they were in trouble. There was no place to hide.

"What do we do?" Vinny whispered.

"Wait it out," Sonny whispered back. "My friends will think of something."

The words were hardly out of his mouth when they were hit with a load of wet, squirming somethings.

One of the fishermen who had just pulled in his net dumped the catch right on the two men totally obliterating them from sight.

"Jesus Christ," Vinny gasped.

"Quiet," Sonny whispered, "No damn Nazi is going to stick his nose in this pile. I told you they'd think of something."

The German made a big show of looking around and moved quickly away from the pile of squirming, wiggling sardines.

When the patrol boat was gone the two Americans shoved their way out of the pile, "Sa bene dia," Sonny smiled. The fisherman smiled back, "Santo, figlio, Santo."

While Sonny and Vinny were crossing the sea, back in Tunisia Hatty began preparations to close headquarters. They would be following the troops to set up a medical station to take care of the casualties.

She was almost finished with her personal packing when a medic came in with a telegram in his hand and shaken look on his face.

"I'm sorry Mrs. Gilbert, but I think you better read this immediately." Hatty looked at his ashen face and knew something terrible had happened.

The telegram was from Thorton. It read...'Come home. Your mother and father were in a fatal accident. Bring Violet.'

Hatty was shaken to the core. No matter how cold or strict they were, they were still her parents and she had to go back to the States.

The next day Hatty and Violet were winging their way across the Atlantic clinging to each other in terrible grief over the tragedy and their lost loves.

Sonny and Vinny arrived at Sciacca just before the break of dawn. The vessel pulled up to an ancient looking ochre colored building and went quickly into a door that opened out on the water.

They walked down a narrow hallway which ended with a door. When they approached the door it opened silently and they went through a dimly lit stone corridor, reminiscent of a cave.

They walked yet to another door which opened when the burly Sicilian knocked three time. They entered a large room , which by it's appearance was a conference room. A large table surrounded by high-backed chairs dominated the room.

At the head of the table sat an aristocratic-looking man dressed in a light beige, well-cut silk suit. His face bore the genes of a Roman senator.

The burly Sicilian bowed to the man, "Sa bene dia Don Pietro."

The man nodded. "Santo." Then he looked at Sonny and Vinny, "These are the two Americans?"

"Yes," The burly man replied, "They have come to pay their respect."

The man nodded again and motioned him to leave. He then turned to Sonny, "Your choice of this young man is commendable."

"Thank you," Sonny replied.

"Have you told him what the conditions are?"

"No, I thought it best that you tell him."

Don Pietro turned to Vinny, "Your Government wants our help to ease the American landings in Sicily. One hand washes the other, right? I do something for you and you do something for me."

Vinny wondered what this cold, steely-eyed man wanted from him and a cold chill went up his spine.

The man, who spoke a learned English, now spoke in the Sicilian language. "I want you to take my daughter out of Sicily and get her to America where she will live with relatives in a place called Lake Tahoe."

Vinny relaxed, then stiffened again. Why did he need him for this job? He wondered.

"Excuse me, Don Pietro, why did you insist on me to accomplish this. Mr. Adams could easily do this far better than me."

"True but Mr. Adams has other things to take care of, important things like winning a war and getting those German bastards out of here."

"Would I be out of line if I ask why the hell you want her out of here?"

The man's eyes closed into small slits. The veins in his neck expanded. His voice was sharp. "My daughter is in a lot of danger. The Germans have discovered her. She's a beautiful, sensuous young lady, headstrong and oblivious to danger to herself and to the rest of us. We have to get her out. These bastards who are supposed to be our allies are treating us like prisoners."

He paused and gave Vinny a long look. "I think she'll go with you without too much complaining." He turned to Sonny, "Are we understood?" Sonny smiled first at Vinny and then at the Don, "Understood."

The Don smiled. "Please accept the hospitality of the Sicilian people and make yourselves comfortable but first, please go take a bath, you both smell like hell," And with that he left.

Vinny looked at Sonny who had a satisfied look on his face, "Is that all? I take the girl back to America?

"And," Sonny crowed, "You stay in America and entertain the soldiers. You can't ask for a better deal than that."

"What about Violet?"

"What about her?"

"I love her God's sake. I don't want to be separated from her."

"This is war kid, you go where you are ordered to go. When the war is over you can get your Violet back, if you're lucky."

The door opened and a man entered, bowed and said, "Follow me."

They were taken to a room that resembled a Roman bath. Showers, whirlpools, steam rooms, massage tables and attendants that catered to them as they showered, sat in the steam room and were massaged. When they finished they were handed their clothes that were washed and freshly pressed.

Then they were ushered through a series of corridors and finally entered a lavishly appointed home…marble floors, thick Persian rugs, tapestries, statues and flowers everywhere. Vinny felt dizzy with all this opulence.

They were greeted by the Don, his sister Donna Lucia and a ravishingly beautiful young girl with raven hair tumbling down and past a petulant face dominated by dark brown velvet eyes.

"This is my sister Donna Lucia and my daughter Gabriella," The Don pointed to each with a look of deep affection on his face.

Sonny and Vinny bowed and said, "Con piacere."

"Speak English," The girl ordered sharply, her pout becoming more exaggerated, "If I must deal with the American barbarians, I might as well start now."

The Don gave her a hard, stern look. Vinny wanted to slap this girl who was probably no older than eighteen. He looked at Sonny whose face remained blank.

"Come," said the Don, "You need some food and rest. Everything is being prepared for your journey tonight."

The bedroom they were assigned to had all the amenities of a rich, lavish home. Vinny looked around him and shook his head in awe.

"Well kid," Sonny grinned, "We'll be ending this gig soon, don't forget to look me up after the war."

"And where will that be?" Vinny asked.

"Some romantic place around here. You won't have trouble finding me."

"Aren't you coming back to the States?"

"Nope, I'm staying here free as a bird. That was part of this deal. They offered it to me and I took it."

That night Sonny, Vinny and a reluctant Gabriella, accompanied by a squad of fishermen returned to Cap Bon.

Back at the hotel in Cap Bon, they turned the girl over to a Tunisian woman and the two men returned to their room in the attic.

We have a couple of days for fun and relaxation," Sonny announced, "Then I go back to Sicily and you kid, go back to America."

Sonny smiled broadly. Vinny's grin was just as wide. "We better get as much loving as we can get and lots of luck to both of us."

Sonny and Vinny headed for the Followers' headquarters and wondered at all the activity when they arrived at the small building.

"Hatty and Violet aren't here," A medic informed them, "They had to fly back to the States."

"Wadda you mean back to the States? What happened?"

"Hatty's parents were killed in an accident," He said sadly. The two ladies were summoned home."

Vinny was stunned. Sonny remained impassive but his heart dropped and he knew that once again he had lost the one love of his life.

Sonny went back to Sicily and worked with the Don to ease the way for the Americans to land on the rugged Sicilian landscape.

Vinny went back to America to escort the petulant Gabriella to Lake Tahoe.

On the plane trip back, Gabriella became talkative and playful. Vinny paid little attention. His mind was on Violet. He was sad but hopeful they would reunite.

'Get her to her relatives fast,' He muttered under his breath, 'And good riddance to bad rubbish.'

As the trip progressed Gabriella began demanding attention.

"Do you have an anomorata?" She queried.

"Yes," Vinny answered curtly.

"When this war is over are you going to marry her?"

"I hope so."

"What do you mean you hope so?"

"She belongs to a religious organization. They don't like Italians," Vinny blurted unconsciously.

"Ah," Gabriella smiled lightly, "So you're not sure."

Vinny looked at the young girl and a chill went up his spine. He turned his head away and Sonny's words came back loud and clear, 'If she marries you, she will be only a wife. Her religion gives her the clout and freedom to travel all over the world, do her good works she was born and raised to do and live high on the hog on other people's money. My advice is to enjoy her while you can.'

Vinny didn't see the conspiratorial smile on Gabriella's face.

Chapter Seventeen

Hatty and Violet arrived home to a scene of total chaos. Joshua had flown in from Portugal where he had been conducting some financial business for the government. This was his war-time work for the government because of his conscientious objectors status.

Thorton was now in total control of the Followers and throwing his weight around shamelessly.

Hatty, in shock, clung to her brother for comfort. Their parents, despite their coldness and strictness, were the solid base of their lives. Violet was bewildered.

They went through the ordeal of a very public funeral, each too stunned to talk.

After the last of the guests departed, Thorton suggested they all retire to the study for the reading of the will.

"I don't think," Hatty cried, "That I can handle it at this time."

Joshua agreed, "Let's wait until tomorrow when we're rested and can think more clearly."

This did not sit well with Thorton. He wanted to get this reading out of the way as quickly as possible. He knew, or thought he knew, that he would inherit the ministry.

Joshua stood his ground and they read the will the following morning.

They sat in the study with one of the followers' lawyers who handled family matters.

Hatty was so miserable at the whole turn of events, her abrupt departure from Sonny, her parents tragic death, a very unhappy and heartbroken Violet, that the reading of the will had little concern for her.

The lawyer cleared his throat and began reading the preliminaries of the legal document. Hatty hardly heard him.

"And now," He continued, "Comes the personal part of your father's last request. "To my son Joshua, I leave the bulk of my estate and he will remain the Followers' Tax Attorney. To my daughter Hatty, I give her sole, behind the scene, power of the

Followers with her husband Thorton as the figure head. She has the final word in all the Followers' affairs."

Thorton was stunned. "What do you mean she has sole, behind the scene power?"

"That's what the will states," Answered the attorney, "What he had in mind I cannot say."

At this Thorton stormed out of the room.

Hatty sat there is stunned silence. Then Joshua started to laugh, "So the old man wasn't as dumb as I thought."

Hatty turned to him, "What do you mean by that?"

"Simply that," Joshua still laughing, "He really knew who the smart and honest person really was. He gave you that power because he realized that under that golden voice, Thorton was a grasping, greedy goose."

Hatty looked around the room and realized Violet had left.

She turned to her brother, "One more thing Josh, are we going to allow that idiot Harper Mills, to marry Violet?"

"As far as I'm concerned, no."

"Good," Hatty replied, "By the way how's Mimi. I knew she couldn't be here and I do want to see her. She's always such a comfort to me."

"I'll tell her, she certainly wants to see you and Violet."

Hatty went looking for Thorton but the maid told her he had gone out. Hatty was relieved. She knew he was going to be difficult to handle but she did hold the winning card and dismissed him from her mind.

She went upstairs to find Violet and found her lying on her bed. She sat down on the bed next to her and put her arms around the grief-stricken girl.

"Tomorrow we'll go to the hat shop and pay Mimi a visit. She's expecting us and don't worry about that idiot Harper Mills, we're not going to let you marry him."

Violet smiled weakly and put her head in Hatty's shoulder, "Oh Auntie, I love Vinny so much."

"Of course you do," Hatty consoled the girl, "And we'll find him, you can bet on that."

The next day the two women went to see Mimi. They hugged and kissed each other warmly. "Tell me everything,"

Mimi begged, "From the day you landed in Africa to the day you left."

Violet's eyes filled with tears. "Oh you poor little lassie, was it that bad?" A worried look crossed Mimi's face.

"Her heart is broken," Hatty moaned, "She's fallen madly in love and now they're apart because of this awful war."

Mimi took Violet's face in her hands, "You mustn't cry beautiful little one, your baby will bring you lots of joy."

"Baby?" Hatty and Violet cried in unison, "What are you talking about?"

"You mean you don't know?" Mimi's face showed horror, "I'm so sorry if I spilled the beans."

Hatty looked at Violet in shock.

Violet's eyes opened wide in disbelief.

"What do you mean, Mimi?" Hatty asked.

Mimi sighed, "It's a gift I have. I can tell if there's a baby inside from the first day of conception." She turned to Violet, "Has your friend visited you this month?"

"I'm due in a couple of days," Violet responded nervously.

"It won't come, lassie. Better get in touch with your sweetie and let him know he's going to be a father." Mimi hugged Violet, "I'm sure the Followers will be very happy to welcome a child of their own member."

Violet and Hatty looked at each other in horror.

Mimi took one look at their faces, crossed herself and murmured softly, "Jesus, Mary and Joseph."

Vinny sighed with relief when he deposited Gabriella at the Lake Tahoe home of her uncle Don Carlo who was a duplicate of his brother Don Pietro.

Anxious to get out of there, Vinny was about to leave when Don Carlo announced that dinner would be served in two hours.

"Thank you but I can't stay," Vinny apologized, "I have to get back to my post."

The Don smiled, "I made arrangements with the post Commander to allow you a weeks leave." Vinny froze. The Don continued, "You will spend the week here and enjoy the hospitality of my home and the pleasure of my niece's company."

Vinny's heart plunged right down to his toes. His throat closed and his heart beat rapidly in anger but he didn't know how to get out of this so-called hospitality.

He was escorted to a bedroom with huge windows overlooking the lake and mountains beyond. If only Violet was here with him. It would be heaven on earth. Instead he felt he had fallen into the fires of hell.

As he walked around the room inspecting the lavish décor, he could not help but wonder how these people made so much money to afford these luxuries.

He was still very angry that the Don cunningly trapped him into staying and to keep that spoiled brat company. 'Well' He fumed, 'If she thought he was going to entertain her, she had another think coming.'

At six on the dot, Vinny answered a soft knock on the door. A big bruiser of a man entered and indicated that Vinny follow him.

They entered the dinning room. Sitting at the head of a big table was Don Carlo. An elegantly dressed woman sat at the other end and at the side sat Gabriella with a smug smile on her face.

"This is my wife, Donna Raffaela," Don Carlo nodded towards the woman.

She nodded to Vinny and motioned him to sit across from Gabriella.

Before he had a chance to unfold his napkin, Donna Raffaela smiled, "I'm happy my niece found such a good-looking young man."

He looked up at her stunned. He didn't see the glow on Gabriella's face.

Anger welled up in him, "Donna Raffaela, I have a girl friend and I intend to marry her."

She looked at him hard, "You intend to marry her but does her religion intend to let her marry you?"

He got up from his chair angrily, "What is this, some kind of conspiracy?"

"Sit down, figlio mia," Donna Raffaela said with a hint of amusement, "We all want the best for our children. We, Don

Carlo and I consider you one of us." She picked up her wine glass and raised it in a toast to Vinny.

"Do you think you'll be happy with this stranger you think you fell in love with? These religious fanatics will make you miserable. Why? Because you're Italian and you're Sicilian. Stay with your own kind and reap the benefits of a close knit family."

Vinny went through the meal so boiling mad, the food, the little he was able to eat went down like lead weights.

"You will excuse me," He said, when the meal was over, "I'm very tired. It's been a rough journey," And without waiting for an answer left the room on the run to his bedroom and slammed the door.

He sat on the bed thoroughly spent. 'How the hell did I get into this situation/' He scowled, 'It looks like one big set-up. I'm going to get out of this if it's the last thing I do.'

He was so exhausted , he fell asleep fully clothed.

At he crack of dawn before he opened his eyes he knew something was wrong. He was under the covers stark naked and lying next to him was Gabriella also without a stitch of clothing.

It took Hatty, Mimi and Joshua all the reserves they had to comfort Violet. The news of Vinny's marriage shocked and horrified Aunt and niece.

Violet's pregnancy put Hatty's network into operation to locate Vinny. The telegram came and sent Hatty reeling. "Sgt. Vincent James of Special Service' It said 'is enjoying a much needed R & R in Miami with his new bride.'

"Perhaps," Joshua counseled "She should marry Harper Mills."

"No, no, no," Hatty and Mimi shouted.

Joshua looked bewildered, "What are we going to do, let her have this baby illegitimately?"

"Yes," Hatty answered sharply, "It's better than living the life I had to live."

Joshua shook his head in agreement, "Whatever you decide Sis, I'm with you."

Hatty smiled, "I'll think of something you can bet on that."

Mimi was gently rocking Violet in her arms whispering soft endearments, "It's alright lassie, everything will work out, God works in mysterious ways," but no amount of consoling could comfort the distraught girl.

Hatty's heart was breaking. She too had suffered a loss. Sonny was gone behind the curtain of war-torn Europe. Would she ever see him again? That's when the solution to Violet's problem popped into her head.

Mimi and Joshua agreed with her and gave their blessing. "Go ahead," Her brother assured her, "I'll take care of the financial part."

Hatty packed up Violet and traveled to New York by train. The apartment in the loft building where Hatty's school –for-the-deaf was located, was a gift from Sonny.

She settled Violet in, then contacted Marty Block, Sonny's solicitor and informed him of her plans.

Violet was to live in the apartment and run the school. Marty hired a maid and companion who would take care of Violet and the baby after it was born. "Sonny always told me, "Marty said, "That anything you wanted, was yours."

"Do you think I will ever see him again?"

"Not in this country, you won't," He shook his head negatively, "But when the war is over you can go and visit him wherever he is."

Marty Block, brilliant lawyer, was a man in his forties. He took care of all of Sonny's legal affaires with discretion and dignity.

He first met Hatty on her first trip to New York when he made all the arrangements for the school and the clandestine meetings between Hatty and Sonny.

Marty and Sonny grew up in the same neighborhood, became friends and though they took different routes in their lives, they loved each other like brothers. He knew how Sonny felt about Hatty and did everything in his power to help her.

She trusted him and knew that Violet would be looked after and made comfortable in her new life.

Vinny wasn't so lucky. After being forced to marry Gabriella, after that brilliant coup, he tried to get away from her as often as possible.

She followed him from base to base and forced herself sexually upon him. He couldn't stand her and was unable to perform at his usual peak. When he did it was with Violet he was making love to.

Gabriella who was cunning as well as selfish knew when Violet came between them.

"Don't worry," Her uncle Don Carlo assured her, "Give him time, he'll forget her."

Gabriella knew better and began looking for sex partners. "My husband," She would sigh, "Is dead between the legs."

She also began throwing tantrums in public, causing a great deal of embarrassment for Vinny and anyone who happened to be around.

There were days when he wanted to kill her. He was so miserable, all he thought about was Violet. Where was she? What was she doing and when was he going to be with her and the end of the brutal separation with the girl he loved.

He vowed that some day, somehow he would free himself from this spoiled, selfish creature who manipulated and tricked him into this loveless marriage.

When he woke up that morning and found her lying next to him, he jumped out of bed and looked for his clothes. They were gone.

He yanked the top sheet off the bed, wrapped himself in it and ran out of the room. He was running to get out of that house.

As he ran down the hall, two burly servants grabbed him and shoved him into Don Carlo's study.

"What the hell is this?" Vinny yelled.

Don Carlo was waiting for him, an angry scowl on his face. "So, you savage my niece and you want to run, huh? Well not so fast young man, we don't stand for that kind of behavior in this family."

"I don't know what the hell you're talking about," Vinny shouted, "I fell asleep with my clothes on. I just woke up, naked,

135

with that girl next to me. I don't know what the hell is going on around here but I didn't do a damn thing to her."

The door opened and Donna Raffaela entered with a tearful Gabriella in tow.

Don Carlo turned to Gabriella, "Well young lady?"

Gabriella turned a tearful face to her uncle. "I'm sorry, Zio but when I passed his room," pointing to Vinny, "He opened the door and dragged me in." She wiped her eyes on the sleeve of her robe, "He told me he was madly in love with me and wanted me so badly, he couldn't wait."

Vinny gasped in horror. "You fucking lying bastard," He screamed.

The two men lunged at him, "Let me go," He shouted, "I never touched her."

Don Carlo raised his hand, "Calm down, we don't raise our voices in this household."

He turned to Gabriella, "Did he take you?"

"Yes," She whispered, "Three times."

Vinny looked at her in disbelief. "She's lying. Boy is she lying. I couldn't have taken her, I was out like a light. Besides, I can't stand her. She's a spoiled, selfish brat. I have a girlfriend I'm madly in love with. I would never go with her, can't you see she's lying."

Don Carlo, in a quiet voice said, "You were in bed with her. You dishonored her and our whole family."

"I did not," Vinny raised his voice again.

Don Carlo ignored him and continued, "You must make up for this terrible thing you did. She's a very beautiful girl and I can understand your desire for her but we can't allow this disgrace to befall our family."

With the two men still holding him, Vinny tried to get out of their grip.

Don Carlo, now an angry look on his face, "No one disgraces this family. There's only one way to make up for this dishonor…"

"And what is that?" Hope coming to him.

"You marry her, otherwise there will be dire consequences."

"You're crazy," Vinny shouted, "She's lying. She tricked me."

The two men gripped him so tightly, Vinny knew what the consequences would be.

Don Carlo waved his hands in dismissal, "Everybody out, except you," He pointed to Vinny.

Vinny was scared now, 'What the hell was this man going to do with me,' He thought. Vinny knew all along that this man was heavily involved in big time racketeering and could eliminate or promote with the snap of his fingers.

"Sit down," The man ordered, a fatherly look now masking his face.

Vinny sat, his knees shaking and his head spinning.

"I was young once," The man smiled, "I know what temptation is."

Vinny interrupted, "I'm trying to tell you I didn't do anything to her."

"It's your word against hers. She was found sleeping with you," He emphasized pointing his finger at Vinny.

Vinny threw his hands up in despair then dropped his head into his hands, "I can't believe this is happening to me. Why? Why? What are you all doing to me?"

"In view of the situation," Don Carlo answered, "You're getting off easy."

"Why don't you just shoot me. My life is already shot."

"If you would just stop feeling sorry for yourself you will see that there is a good side to this."

"Such as?" Vinny asked almost in tears.

"Listen to me," Don Carlo ordered gently, "Accept this marriage and you will realize all your dreams...a successful career on the stage and movies...a life of luxury and a life of ease for your mother."

"My mother?" Vinny almost croaked, "What do you know about my mother?"

The older man smiled. "She lives in a shabby, run down tenement on tenth Avenue, works as a seamstress and hardly makes ends meet."

Vinny was stunned. "How the hell do you know all this about my mother and how in the hell can you make her life easy?"

The older man leaned back in his chair, "We make it our business to know everything. How can we make her life easy? Simple. We take her out of that rat hole and put her in one of our town houses on Washington Square. There she'll live without any cares or worries and she can grow her flowers and tomatoes in the back yard garden instead of that rusty fire escape."

Vinny loved his mother and the one thing he always vowed was to get her out of the tenement. He knew he was trapped and if this meant that his mother would live in comfort, so be it.

Vinny and Gabriella were married in a lavish Roman Catholic Church with an equally lavish reception at one of the best hotels in Lake Tahoe.

The war raged on. The Sicilian invasion was carried out and the American soldiers found themselves fighting the Germans as the Italian soldiers surrendered en masse to the American troops.

Sonny's mission was successful.

He set up headquarters in the remote hills of Sicily helping the Americans as they made their way across the rugged mountainous landscape.

The German's every move was relayed to the American Generals, thus easing, what was an almost impossible path to Messina.

With Sicily finally in the hands of the Allies, Sonny settled into a villa on a small estate tucked in the crevices of the treacherous mountains of central Sicily.

Here he had easy access to the busy cities of Palermo, Messina, Agrigento and Syracusa, where he conducted his private business.

He never lost his power. If any, it increased. But through this all, his mind and heart went back to Hatty. Sometimes his longing for her was so overpowering he was tempted to flee the country and sneak into the U.S.

There was a parade of women who took care of his physical needs but his heart never stopped bleeding.

Hatty, back in the mid-west, was dealing with the administration of the Followers, keeping in constant touch with Violet and keeping Thorton in front of the people and discreetly keeping his male friends at a distance.

Thorton was angry but Hatty held the winning cards and he knew if he wanted to keep his life style, he had to obey her orders.

How he hated her. They never ate together except for formal dinners with high ranking members of the Followers, bankers, political figures and big-money donors.

On the surface they presented a handsome, loving couple, highly respected by everyone.

Every time she spoke to Marty Block in New York, she asked the same question, "Have you had any word?" And Marty would reply, "When I do, I'll let you know immediately."

Violet in the meantime kept busy with the school and took long walks as her pregnancy progressed.

She walked around the village exploring the quaint shops and bustling restaurants and was always amazed at the diversity of the city; it's people; it's culture and the acceptance of each other's differences.

She especially liked to sit in Washington Square Park and watch the parade of soldiers, and marines as they mingled with the artistic Bohemians. And her heart never stopped crying.

She was at her desk. The snow was falling in large flakes when she felt the first sharp pain.

She immediately called Hatty but was told her Aunt was out in the field and couldn't be reached.

She then called Mimi who told her to call Marty Block. Mimi, who loved Violet as if she were her real niece, assured the laboring girl that everything was going to be taken care of and that Hatty and she would come out to New York to be with her.

Violet gave birth to a beautiful eight pound seven ounce girl and instantly named her Cheri, the French word for darling.

It was the name her fun-loving father, Preston Gilbert, called her mother, his French, Chinese, Russian wife.

The baby had both Violet and Vinny in her. His cleft chin, her almond-shaped eyes with Vinny's chameleon color. The baby also inherited his dark curly hair.

Ever since she arrived in New York to run the school-for-the-deaf and have her –out-of – wed-lock baby, Violet kept her love for Vinny locked in her heart.

She never forgot that awful day when her Aunt Hatty and Mimi gave her the news that Vinny was married.

"To whom?" She cried, "He never mentioned a girl back home. He told me he loved me and couldn't wait for the war to end so that we could join each other in Holy Matrimony.

"An Italian girl," Hatty responded sadly, "Something about an arranged marriage."

Violet cried uncontrollably. The shock of finding out she was pregnant and the news of Vinny's marriage, was too much to take.

Would she ever forget Vinny? Never, she told herself, not with Cheri reminding her every minute of the day.

Violet was nursing the baby and her thoughts went back to her own early childhood. How happy she was in the loving care of her beautiful mother and her handsome, spirited father.

Tears filled her eyes. Cheri would never have the pleasure of her handsome father's love.

"Why?" She cried, "Was life so cruel to her?" Her parents were brutally snatched from her when she was only three years old and now her own beautiful baby without a father."

Marty Block kept her hospital room filled with flowers and visited her every morning.

He came in on the third day of her confinement with a big grin on his face.

"I've a big surprise for you," He laughed, "Look who's here."

Violet screeched with delight as Hatty and Mimi walked into the room.

There were hugs and kisses and tears as Violet clung to the two most important people in her life.

At last the baby was brought in and Hatty almost lost her breath. There was enough of Vinny in the baby, features that would be a constant reminder of a lost love.

When all the excitement died down, Violet with a worried frown on her face asked Hatty, "Does Uncle Thorton know about the baby?"

"Of course he does," Hatty replied, "But he doesn't know about Vinny. You know how he would react. A New York Italian."

"What did you tell him?"

Hatty laughed. "I told him some soldier spiked your ginger ale and seduced you while you were out cold."

"Aunt Hatty," Violet cried, "How could you?"

"Easy," Her Aunt smiled, "I don't want him holding a sword over my head."

"What did he say when you told him that?"

"Nothing, he just snorted."

"Oh Auntie what if he finds out the truth?"

"He won't. There was too much going on during that period. The only ones who know about Vinny is Sonny, Mimi, Uncle Josh and me. You don't have to worry about us."

Life went on as the war escalated until that fateful day in April when Germany surrendered and later in August when Japan surrendered on the battleship Missouri.

Violet's life settled down as she juggled her life as a single mother.

She ran the school quietly and efficiently and nurtured the baby with the help of a competent and loving nanny.

Violet included in her busy schedule, walking the baby every afternoon. She loved pushing the carriage around the neighborhood and the park.

There she met young mothers with their babies and some older women who had grandchildren elsewhere and indulged in grandmotherly love with the babies in the park.

She loved talking to them and when asked about the baby's father, she always replied, as Hatty had instructed her, that he died in the war.

This elicited a lot of sympathy. One older woman, in particular always sought her out to coo and admire the baby.

She spoke softly in Italian. Violet couldn't understand her, but she loved looking at this woman's arresting face. A face that was finely chiseled and dominated by translucent gray eyes.

She would look down at Cheri and murmur something in Italian. The expression on her face was a mixture of puzzlement and longing.

One day Violet said to her, "What's your name?"

"Rosina," The woman replied, "And yours?"

"My name is Violet."

"Ah, Violetta, che bella nome." Pointing to the baby, "E la bambina?"

"Cheri," Violet answered smiling.

"Un bella nome per una bella bambina," And looked down at the baby again with that puzzled look on her face.

Violet always left the park with a strange surreal feeling after these encounters with Rosina.

Hatty made frequent trips to New York and always engaged in long private conversations with Marty Block.

"What do you two have to talk about?" Violet asked, "I hope it's not about me."

"Yes, we do discuss you sweetheart, because we all love you and the baby so much but we do have a lot of other business to talk about, one very important subject is the school."

"I'm sorry," Violet apologized, "I won't ask any more questions because I know you need your privacy.""

Hatty hugged Violet, "Our hearts have been badly shattered but we're survivors and we will come out of this splendidly."

Violet always missed Hatty terribly after one of these trips and the two kept the telephone lines busy.

Hatty arrived one day in a state of excitement. After a session with Marty Block, Hatty announced she was taking a short trip to Cuba.

"Cuba?" Violet asked surprised, "What are you going to do in Cuba?"

Hatty winked at Violet, "I'm going to case the joint."

"Oh Auntie," Violet laughed, "You are so funny."

Marty drove Hatty to nearby Teterboro Airport in New Jersey where she boarded a small Cessna and took off for the tropical island of Cuba.

She settled down to a quiet time during the five hour flight, to reflect over her life as it was before Sonny and what it had become after Sonny.

'It was incredible,' she mused, 'how one person changed her life. In her case it was two. The arrival of Violet and the day Sonny walked into her life.

Violet changed her life like a slowly opening rose bud. Sonny like a flaming orange bolt of lightening.

Everything he did had a heightened sense of excitement. The way he looked at her with those mysterious, smoldering black eyes.

His gentleness under that rough exterior. His knowledge of almost every subject. And most of all, his sexuality which always satisfied but always called for more.

She wondered about his relationship with Vinny. Would he be able to tell her why the young, handsome soldier, who was so in love with Violet would suddenly marry someone else?

And Violet, her beautiful young niece whose heart was so wounded that it would take a lifetime to repair, if ever.

And the beautiful Cheri who bore a lot of her father's looks.

Did she do the right thing by not letting Violet marry a man who would give the baby legitimacy?

All these thoughts crowded her mind as she raced above the clouds for a rendezvous with love.

The small plane landed lightly in a small airport outside of Havana. Hatty stepped into a waiting limo and was whisked off to a small isolated villa high in the hills above the bustling city.

The gates to the estate closed behind her and there standing on the steps to the mansion was Sonny looking more splendid than ever.

He came flying down the steps, picked her off her feet and hugged her with sheer joy.

"Oh Hatty," He sighed, "You will never know how much I longed for you."

Hatty busy kissing his lips, his eyes, his cheeks, laughed and cried. "My heart was always with you. Night and day. Week after week. Month after month."

"Let me look at you," He laughed, holding her at arms length. "God, you're more beautiful than ever." He hugged her tightly, "I love you Hatty. I love you so much."

The servants stood slightly behind him and smiled broadly. He turned to them, "Isn't she beautiful?"

"Si, Senor, si senor," They nodded, "Mucho linda."

"Come," He said "We've prepared a big feast, but first let me take you to your room," He bent down and whispered, "We must show some decorum in front of the servants," And laughed heartily.

He ushered her into the bedroom and dismissed the servants. "They'll take care of things while we're eating."

The long separation and the years of longing exploded. They undressed each other with passionate fury and were encased in each other's arms demanding and receiving succor with a desperation resulting from a long absence.

After a sumptuous meal of Caribbean and Italian food, they went into the living room for coffee.

They settled comfortably onto large overstuffed sofas.

"I know you want to ask me something," His face showing concern, "It's all over your face."

She put her cup down on the coffee table, looked at him with pain in her eyes, "Why did Vinny suddenly marry someone else?"

He put his cup down softly. "It's very complicated Hatty. I hope you will understand."

"Sonny, there's a baby involved. A beautiful little girl who will remind her every day of her life of a love she lost in a way she can't understand, and a baby who is growing up without the love of her father."

He got down on his knees before her and took her hands. "I swear, I thought it was a war-time infatuation. If I had known I would have replaced him for that very important mission."

"Start from the beginning," Hatty pleaded. "Tell me everything if you can and then you and I will try to repair the damages."

Sonny loved Hatty with an intense passion and deep concern. He worried about her loveless relationship with the greedy, ambitious Thorton. Were their infrequent, physical and clandestine meetings enough for her? She was a sensuous woman and being with her was always exciting and even spiritual. How much should he tell her? Would she understand the terrible pressures they were under to get the mission accomplished?

Hatty had grown tremendously in stature and spirit since that day he went to her house for dinner. He trusted her no-nonsense approach to life's problems.

They settled down facing each other as he revealed the strange, incredible account that brought Sonny to Africa and why they chose Vinny as the important link in this chain of events.

Hatty listened quietly and intently interrupting him only occasionally when something sounded bizarre to her.

"But why him? There were so many handsome young Italian-American soldiers in that theatre of operations."

"True, but have you seen any with his unusual qualities?"

She shook her head.

"A person's character is molded from the day he's born. Vinny's parents, were in a sense, show people appearing in front of the public. He's a natural-born showman. Coupled with extraordinary good looks and the ability to handle himself in front of high profile people, made him the perfect candidate for the job."

Hatty took a sip of coffee, "And?"

"The mission would not have been possible without his help."

"Why was that?"

"Because no deal would have been made if we didn't take the capo's daughter out of the country."

"And you needed Vinny to do that?"

"Yes, we had to get the most handsome G.I. we could get our hands on. And he was it."

145

Hatty put down her cup, "Oh, Sonny I can take it. There's a lot more to this than that."

"There certainly is," Sonny replied, "That girl is a bundle of dynamite, headstrong, spoiled, selfish and very beautiful. She attracts men like bees to a honey pot."

"And she wasn't going to go along with the plot unless there was something in it for her."

Sonny looked at Hatty with pain in his eyes. "How right you are. She was meeting with the Germans blatantly and was becoming a danger to everyone around her. Getting her out was the Capo's main desire. So we had to find someone she would be willing to go with and that's where Vinny came into the picture."

"Did you know that marriage was on everyone's mind?"

"Yes, but I told you before, I thought his love for Violet was merely a war-time infatuation."

"Now what do we do?"

"Do you trust me, Hatty?"

"Of course I do."

"Then leave everything to me. It might take some time but Violet and the baby will get Vinny back. That I promise you."

Chapter Eighteen

When the war in Europe ended Vinny went to his commanding officer and requested to be immediately sent to the Pacific. His comedic talent, his good looks and his smooth singing voice were noticed by much of the army brass.

Requests for his performances were coming in from camps all over the country. His hatred for Gabriella was so strong that he preferred going to the islands and jungles of the Pacific than be anywhere near her.

At first his request was refused but at his insistence he was flown first to Hawaii then to the islands the Americans had recaptured.

He was hoping that somehow Violet would be among the medics now in the Pacific.

As soon as the plane hit the runway, his hopes high, he was off to check out the medical units. His disappointments sent him into despair.

On August third, nineteen forty five, on the battleship Missouri, a peace pact was signed and World War II came to an end.

It was time to go home. Vinny wrestled with his conscious. Where was home? Lake Tahoe where hell reigned supreme or New York where his mother was living a comfortable life.

His mother never understood his marriage to the beautiful, spoiled Italian girl and her move from her tenth avenue tenement to the lovely town house on Washington Square.

She wondered and worried but kept her counsel. The strange story would unravel someday, somehow.

Vinny decided on New York. There in the big, bustling city of his birth the solution to his problem would be decided.

Vinny arrived at his mother's Washington Square house on a cold December day as dusk was falling on the city.

He rang the bell, knocked on the big front door at the top of the steps but received no answer. Not having a key he sat on the steps of the big stoop and waited.

He looked up and down the street, a worried look on his face. He wondered where she could be on this cold day. Suddenly she came around the corner walking beside a girl with a carriage.

He thought he was having hallucinations. He readily recognized his mother. The girl threw him for a loop. His heart was racing. Every girl, from afar, resembled Violet.

He sighed and waited for the two females who were busy chatting, and never noticed the handsome, young soldier sitting on the stoop.

Suddenly Rosina looked up and let out a joyous cry, "Figlio mio," And was immediately embraced in the arms of her son.

Hugging, kissing and caressing his face, the tears stinging her eyes, she did not see Violet's reaction.

Vinny turned to greet the girl, grabbed the railing to keep from falling. Stunned and paralyzed, he stared at Violet and the carriage in disbelief.

"Oh my God," Vinny cried, "Violet, oh my God."

In an instant they were wrapped in each other's arms. Then they drew back away from each other as reality set in.

Vinny pointed to the carriage, "You're married?"

"No," Violet sobbed, "But you are."

Rosina looked bewildered. How did her son know this girl? Why did they fly into each other's arms? Was she a friend of his? Did he know her husband?

"Vincenzo," Rosina cried, "How do you know this girl? Who is she?"

Vinny turned to his mother, put his arms around her, tears streaming down his face, "Mama, this is Violet, the woman I was supposed to marry."

"But you married the girl from Italy."

"I know Mama, I know. I didn't want to marry her. It's a long story."

He turned to Violet, "Whose baby is this? Are you taking care of her for someone?"

Violet shook her head. Tears rolled down her face. "I can't tell you Vinny, please don't ask me."

"Why not?"

Rosina stepped in. "It's her baby, that's what she told me."

"Is that true?"

"It's true," Violet trembled, "She's mine."

"Whose the father?"

"It doesn't matter," Violet's voice quivered.

"Violet for heavens sake, tell me. Despite all that has happened, I love you. I'll always love you. It's you I wanted, not that idiot they roped me into marrying."

"I can't tell you Vinny and I won't. I must protect my baby."

She turned the carriage around and started to leave. Rosina put her hand on the carriage and stopped it from moving.

"From the first day I looked at this baby I saw my Vincenzo. How could this stranger's baby, I ask myself, look so much like my boy? I thought I must be seeing things that weren't there. In my heart I felt this baby was mine that's why I always made sure I was in the park when Violet came in."

She turned to Vinny, "Ask her again."

Vinny went to the carriage, looked down at the sleeping baby and the photograph of him as a child appeared instantly on the sleeping infant's face.

"Oh my God, why are you denying this?"

Violet's face, so full of pain, murmured, "It's too late Vinny. We tried to contact you and found out you were on your honeymoon."

Rosina bent over the carriage, reached in, picked up the baby and cradled the infant in the warmth of her arms.

"Dio mio," Tears rolled down her cheeks. Tears of joy and sadness showed on her face.

Vinny took the baby from his mother and gently hugged the little child he knew was his.

"I'll never let you go, my little sweetheart," He cooed, "Never. Your mother and I will always be with you. I'll get this mess straightened out."

"Let's go inside," Rosina smiled through her tears. "I want to really see my grandchild."

Inside the townhouse, Cheri's heavy snowsuit and hood was removed revealing a child reminiscent of a Michaelangelo fresco.

Violet dried her tears and wondered where this was all going. He was married. She had no legal right to him. Her heart ached as she looked at the man who had loved her so passionately then ran off with another woman.

"I must go," She stammered, "I can't stay here."

"Sit down Violet," Vinny pleaded, "You have to hear the story. You too Mama."

They listened quietly wiping their eyes as they heard the incredible story unfold.

"Listen to me, both of you," Vinny's voice hard and determined, "I'm going to untangle this mess. First I have to find the person who dumped me into this hell."

Vinny insisted on walking Violet and the baby home. "She's mine," He kept saying, "Dear God, she's mine."

Coming out of Violet's building was Marty Block.

"This is Vinny," A tearful, shaken Violet spoke.

Marty smiled broadly, extended his hand, "I know, I'm Sonny Adams friend and lawyer. Take Violet and the baby upstairs, then meet me at the bar," Pointing to a neighborhood tavern situated at the corner of the street "We have some things that have to be discussed."

An hour later Vinny left the tavern and returned to Violet's flat. He took her in his arms and held her, kissing her face, her lips, her eyes. "You have no idea how many times I dreamed of holding you in my arms and never letting you go."

Violet collapsed in his arms and let confused emotions take over her body and mind.

The next morning, Vinny and Rosina were sitting at the kitchen table eating breakfast. "What are you going to do?" She asked, a troubled look on her face.

"Whatever we have to do to get out of this mess," Vinny responded, a determined look on his face.

They both fell silent, each in their troubled thoughts when the front doorbell rang.

"It's eight o'clock," Vinny puzzled, "Who can that be?"

"I don't know," Rosina, just as puzzled answered, "I'm not expecting anyone. The cleaning lady is coming tomorrow."

"I'll get it," Vinny got up. He opened the door and standing there in all her brazen good looks was Gabriella.

"Well aren't you going to let me in?" Her face showing impatience and temper.

"What the hell are you doing here?" Vinny almost shouted.

"I stopped by to see my so-called husband," Gabriella sneered. "I do have a legal right to see my husband, no?"

Vinny opened the door, Gabriella pushed past him and walked towards Rosina who was standing in the kitchen doorway, a look of frantic disbelief on her face.

"Don't worry," Gabriella tossed her long, raven hair, "I'm not staying, I'm on my way to Cuba."

"Cuba?"

"Uh huh. I'm on my way to a brand new life where there's lots of action, beautiful tropical breezes, not like that ice-cold Lake Tahoe, and a part ownership in a casino hotel."

Vinny was speechless.

"Oh close your mouth," She scolded, "I came to offer you a job entertaining in one of my night clubs. I don't know if they'll appreciate your talents, I know I never did, but I feel generous."

"Please," Rosina pleaded, "Let him go so he can stay with his bambina."

"A baby? Well, well. When did this happen? Did you forget your Holy Roller girlfriend so soon? A girl you were so crazy about you couldn't make love to me."

Vinny's anger welled up in him, "She's the Holy Roller, as you put it, the mother of my baby. It happened in Tunisia just before I went to Sicily and had the misfortune to have met you."

"Too bad," Gabriella smiled wickedly, "we're Italians, we don't get divorces. It's against the Church Laws, remember?"

His heart went down to the pit of his stomach. Then he stood up straight, hope showing in his face. "I don't give a damn about Church Laws. I'll get a divorce whether you like it or not."

"We'll see," Gabriella laughed, "I don't lose easily or quietly." She handed him a business card, "Call me every once in a while, dear husband, and when you smarten up I'll hire you to entertain my guests."

She tuned to Rosina, "Try talking some sense into that stupid son of yours." She looked around the well-appointed house and stated gleefully, "I see you quickly got accustomed to the good life. Bye, Bye," And was out the door and gone before the astonished mother and son could answer her.

They were still standing in shock when the doorbell rang again.

Vinny opened the door. Marty Block saw the bewildered look on the young man's face. He motioned mother and son into the kitchen.

"I know this looks bad," Marty spoke softly, "But everything will come out alright."

"You don't know what she's like," Vinny shook his head, "She spoiled rotten and she comes from a powerful family. Whatever she wants, she gets."

Marty nodded his head in agreement," True but the whole situation has been explained and amendments are being made."

He took Vinny's hands, "Just be patient." He reached into his breast pocket, "By the way, I have a message for you. It seems a Broadway producer saw you perform in Hawaii. He tracked you down here."

Vinny looked puzzled.

Marty laughed. "He wants you to audition for a role in a musical he's putting together. Go for it, kid, he told me you are a natural."

Vinny still looked worried, "What about my mother. This house?"

Marty laughed again, "This house is one of Sonny's properties. He owes you kid. He owes you big. Mama stays here, thanks to you."

Violet had just finished feeding Cheri when the door burst open and Hatty, Mimi and Joshua walked in.

"Oh my sweetheart," Hatty cooed, "He's back."

Violet with tears in her eyes nestled into her Aunt's arms holding back sobs. "He's married Auntie, he can't come back."

Mimi and Joshua gathered around the Aunt and niece comforting the young girl.

"Oh yes he can sweetheart," Joshua consoled, "He's got a lot of people on his side. You'll get him back," He assured her, "Love pulls many strings." They all laughed hugging and kissing Violet and Cheri.

Mimi, her mop of red hair, escaping from the cloche hat on her head, chimed, "Where is this handsome hunk of man who has stolen you heart, Violet?"

As if on cue, the door bell rang. Hatty opened the door and ushered in Vinny and Rosina.

Introductions were made. The baby, nestled cozily in Rosina's arms, cooed merrily.

"See," Rosina smiled broadly, "She's with family,"

Vinny held Violet in his arms and vowed they would get rid of the terrible creature and start living his life in the glow of Violet' love.

They all settled down and each in his and her mind wondered if the road to happiness was to remain as rocky, bumpy and full of obstacles.

After all it was love that kept them going.

Epilogue

Life moved on. Would Hatty ever live a normal life with the man she loved? Would Violet survive the trauma of her tragic life? They told her everything would work out, but would it? Would Mimi and Joshua ever legalize their passionate love for each other? And Vinny, where is he headed in this dangerous entanglement? Let's not forget Thorton...his greed and ambitions.

Only destiny, the choreographer of life knew where their paths would go.

About the Author

Phyllisanne Pisano is a former New York City Retail Advertising Copywriter and Community Dinner Theatre Publicist. She also writes about the Italian-American experience in articles and tele-plays. She lives with her husband Anthony in Northern New Jersey.